THE UNITED STATES, SLAVERY AND THE SLAVE TRADE IN THE NILE VALLEY

Ahmed E. Elbashir

UNIVERSITY PRESS OF AMERICA

LANHAM • NEW YORK • LONDON

University Press of America,™ Inc.

4720 Boston Way
Lanham, MD 20706

3 Henrietta Street
London WC2E 8LU England

Printed in the United States of America

ISBN (Perfect): 0-8191-3491-0
ISBN   (Cloth): 0-8191-3490-2

To Joellen, Tarik, and Hanadi.

iv

Acknowledgements

I am deeply indebted to a number of people for their assistance. Special thanks go to Dr. Merze Tate, Professor-Emeritus of History, Howard University; and to Dr. Hassan Ibrahim of the Department of History, University of Khartoum, both of whom reviewed the manuscript and offered valuable remarks and observations.

I also wish to thank the staffs of the National Archives, Washington, D.C.; the Library of Congress; the Moorland-Spingarn Research Center, Howard University; and Sudan Archives, all of whom were most helpful and paved the way for my fruitful research at their institutions.

Finally, I wish to express my appreciation to the University of Juba in Sudan, which made possible my trip to the Sudan in the summer of 1979 by inviting me to lecture there.

CONTENTS

PREFACE ix

INTRODUCTION: SLAVERY AND THE SLAVE TRADE
                 IN THE NILE VALLEY   1

                  PART ONE:

                PUBLIC REACTIONS

   I. The Invisible Connection: The Hamitic Myth . 19

  II. American Travelers in the Nile Valley:
      Impressions and Conceptions 27

      Pre-Civil War Travelers to Egypt   28
      Pre-Civil War Travelers to Sudan   35
      Post-Civil War Travelers to Egypt and Sudan   37

 III. The Molding of Public Opinion 45

      The White Press   46
      The Black Press and the Mahdia   56

  IV. American Missionaries and Soldiers: Envoys
      of Modernization 61

      The American Mission in Egypt   61
      American Officers in the Egyptian Army   66
      The Union versus the Confederacy in Egypt   73

                  PART TWO:

             THE OFFICIAL RESPONSE

   V. The Nile Valley and the American Civil War . 79

      The Cotton Boom in Egypt   80
      Sudanese Soldiers in Mexico   81

VI. From Indifference to Procrastination . . .   91

    William Thayer, American Consul-General,
      Alexandria, 1861-1863   91
    Charles Hale, American Consul-General,
      Alexandria, 1864-1870   93
    Richard Beardsley, American Consul-General,
      Alexandria, 1873-1874   98

VII. Elbert Eli Farman, American Consul-General
    in Cairo, 1876-1881   111

    Conflicting Signals from Washington   111
    Farman Envisions a U.S. Role   117

VIII. The Mahdia and the United States: Reactions
    and Interpretations   131

    Consular Despatches Concerning the Mahdia   132
    British Occupation of the Sudan   136

CONCLUSION   139

APPENDICES   143

    A: Letter to the U.S. Secretary of State,
        William H. Seward from U.S. Consul-
        General in Egypt, William S. Thayer   143

    B: Convention Between Egypt and Great
        Britain for the Suppression of the
        Slave Trade, 1877   145

    C: Convention Between Great Britain and
        Egypt for the Suppression of Slavery
        and the Slave Trade, 1895   149

    D: Consular Officers by Post: Egypt 1835-
        1899   155

NOTES   157

SOURCES   175

INDEX   185

PREFACE

The Nile Valley, as far as this study is concerned, comprises the present-day United Arab Republic of Egypt and the Democratic Republic of the Sudan.

Several studies have attempted in the past to compare the United States' efforts to abolish the trans-Atlantic slave trade to those of Great Britain, especially in their joint venture of the African Squadron, 1843-1862. The United States emerged as delinquent in each. Such comparisons were both unfair and unjustifiable because they overlooked an important fact--that the United States was a slave society, while Great Britain was not, despite the fact that it had profited immensely from the traffic.

This study purports to give a panoramic view of the attitudes of the United States government, religious leaders, and the American public in general toward the question of the slave trade and slavery in the Nile Valley, in juxtaposition to the attitudes of their counterparts in the region itself. By doing so, the study substitutes the old emphasis with a new one of comparing the actions and attitudes of one slave society with those of another.

Little has been written on the subject of American-Nile Valley relations in the nineteenth century; and amazingly, such studies that do exist fail to discuss the subject of the American reaction to slavery, even though the same corpus of official documents is utilized. The fact that those who examined the records were either American or Egyptian scholars gives a clue to the reason for their convenient avoidance of the unpleasant subject.

The sources of this study are three: the correspondence between the United States Consuls-General in Egypt and the State Department; the books written by contemporary American travelers to the region, and scholars interested in the newly-acclaimed ancient civilization of Egypt, as well as the origin of the region's populace; and American newspapers. These sources contain a wealth of information about the American soul-searching as a result of contact with another slave society during one of its most turbulent periods in the nineteenth century. The fact that they were not intentionally written to expose this aspect make them the more revealing and useful to serve the purposes of this study.

The fact that the study concerns itself with reactions and interpretations rather than policies and positions places it in that gray area between diplomatic history and social history. It is divided into two sections, the first dealing with the unofficial reaction; the second dealing with the official. It is therefore organized along these two lines, with occasional overlapping.

A summary and the conclusion of this study were introduced in the Graduate Seminar of the History Department, University of Khartoum, Sudan, and at the University's Institute of African and Asian Studies, both in the summer of 1979. Parts of Chapter VIII, concerning the Mahdia and American reactions and interpretations of it, were delivered as a paper at the International Centennial Conference of the Mahdia, sponsored by the History Department, University of Khartoum in November of 1981. Each presentation was followed by stimulating discussions which helped the writer in preparing this manuscript.

INTRODUCTION

SLAVERY AND THE SLAVE TRADE IN THE NILE VALLEY

By the beginning of the nineteenth century slavery
and the slave trade were deep-rooted institutions in
Egypt and Northern Sudan. Two types of slave trade
were discernable in the region. The first and more
extensive was in the indigenous black slaves captured
on the southern peripheries of Northern Sudan, mainly
the Nuba Mountains, Northern Bahr al-Ghazal, the Sobat
River, and the Ethiopian-Sudanese borders. The second
type was limited and less pervasive. It was in white
slaves obtained from Anatolia (modern Turkey),
Circassia, in the Black Sea region, Georgia in the
Caucasus, and from southeast Europe; and brown slaves
purchased from Abyssinia (modern Ethiopia) mainly from
the Aromo tribe.

Egypt was both exporting black slaves and importing
white and brown slaves. Northern Sudan absorbed a
sizable portion of its black captives and exported the
rest to Egypt and Arabia.

For thousands of years the central state in Egypt
and later, in Northern Sudan, had preyed on its decen-
tralized southern black neighbors. The coming of Islam
had enforced rather than initiated the slave trade
patterns already evolving in the Nile Valley. The
demand for black slaves was expanded as a result of
the region being part of a wider Islamic market. The
well-established tradition of capturing slaves from
the less centralized black tribes on the peripheries
was further consolidated and rationalized by the fact
that they were "pagans." This religious dimension was
an Islamic augmentation.

The scarcity of land in Egypt and the existence
of a well-trained, docile class of peasants (fellaheen),
precluded the use of slaves for farm labor. Instead,
slaves had been used in Egypt since time immemorial
in the armies as retainers and soldiers, and in households for menial service and pleasure. The fact that
Islam permitted four wives and an unlimited number of
concubines gave those who could afford the luxury the
incentive to own as many slaves as their finances
permitted.

The ruling and wealthy elites kept harems, where
eunuchs were employed to serve them. Eunuchs were
primarily blacks, and were especially in demand in Egypt.

1

Coptic monks in remote monasteries specialized in
running the eunuch factories. Young boys were chosen
and operated on by the monks. There were three types
of operations: removal of the genitals; removal of
the penis; and removal of the testicles. Because
of the high mortality rate among those operated on,
the prices of eunuchs were several times higher than
those of their counterparts.

A hierarchy evolved among the slaves, with young
white females on the top, and black males at the
bottom. Eunuchs and brown Abyssinian females were in
between, with the black female trailing them. Needless
to add that the same hierarchy based on color existed
in Egyptian society. In the intrigues of the palaces,
and in the absence of any rigid system of succession
to the throne, the eunuchs often played extremely
influential roles, more than once unsurping the throne
and ruling supreme, for example, the black, Kafur,
who ruled Egypt indirectly as Regent, and directly
from A.D. 946-968.

The same hierarchy based on color and race
prevailed among slave soldiers. The white ones, referred
to as Mamluks, "owned ones," were given special training
and groomed for positions in special elite forces.
Black slave soldiers, referred to as abeed, "slaves,"
were recruited casually and constituted the rank and
file of the Egyptian troops. Clashes between the two
groups were frequent. The ascendancy of the Mamluks
to power in Egypt in A.D. 1250-1517 had placed them
firmly as the ruling elites. They ruled Egypt
effectively as an oligarchy, and played an important
role in repelling the Crusaders. After 1517, they
continued to play an important military role under the
Ottoman Empire. In 1798, they were defeated by
Napoleon Bonaparte, who was defeated in turn by the
British, interested in the overland Suez route to
India.

In Northern Sudan, black slaves were used on
farms by the rivrain and semi-nomadic tribes. The
gradual penetration of Islam in the region, mainly
through the migration of displaced Arab tribes from
Upper Egypt, had created after the ninth century an
uneven spread of the two processes of islamization and
arabization. These two processes cemented the traditional cultural ties of the region with North Africa
and the Middle East, while weakening its relations
with the rest of the tropical Africa.

Early in the nineteenth century, Russian annexation of the Caucasian lands, 1801-28, reduced the supply of white slaves to the Islamic World, resulting in the increased demand for black slaves. The ancient law of supply and demand effected the Nile Valley. The conquest of the Sudan, though also prompted by other reasons, coincided with this development.[1] The aggressive and entrepreneuring class of slave traders in the islamized and arabized Northern Sudan increased their efforts to meet the rising need both in the region and abroad.

The millenia of intermixture which had taken place between North African and Middle Eastern migrating groups had created all shades of non-white colors in Northern Sudan. The criteria of color and race used in Egypt to differentiate between the Egyptians and the imported slaves on one hand, and between the slaves themselves on the other, were not tenable in Northern Sudan. The emphasis, therefore, was primarily on arabism and islamism. Thus the ancient slave trade took on an ethno-religious character. The slave-hunting expeditions were called ghazwas, "jihad against pagans." However, it is essential to differentiate between the teaching of Islam and its practice in Northern Sudan.

* * *

When Mohammed Ali Pasha (1769-1849), the Viceroy of Egypt, decided to conquer the Sudan in 1820, his primary motive was to recruit black slaves for his army. Seeking to create a strong, modernized army in order to achieve his independence from the Ottoman Empire, and to build a Middle Eastern empire of his own, Mohammed Ali looked to Sudan for the supply of slaves and mercenary toops who were reputed for their courage and stamina.

Northern Sudan, except for Darfur, was easily over-run by the invading Turco-Egyptian army. Slaves were captured and sent to Upper Egypt to be trained by French officers. The high rate of mortality among them, and their unpreparedness for rigorous military training, turned Mohammed Ali Pasha's grand plan of a black army into an utter failure. He did not abandon the Sudan, however, in spite of the fact that, contrary to contemporary prevailing rumors, the region was poor in metals, particularly gold.

The traditional slave trade continued under the Turco-Egyptian administration on a wider scale. Two new factors were responsible. First, relatively heavy taxes had been imposed on the impoverished Northern Sudanese tribes. In the absence of cash, taxes were paid in slaves. The Turco-Egyptian officials and soldiers were also paid in slaves. The slave hunting groups increased and intensified their efforts to meet the imperatives of the new situation. Second, annual expeditions were organized by the government itself to obtain slaves to replenish its black garrisons, and to increase its revenues. Side by side with this official involvement, and because of it, individual officials of all ranks moonlighted as slave traders themselves in order to supplement their low salaries. Most of them were banished to work in the Sudan as punishment.

The opening of the Sudan and the lucrative slave trade attracted many European and Levantine adventures. The fact that the Sudan was remote from the seat of power in Egypt made it an ideal place for their involvement in the slave trade.

In 1839-1841 the Sudd ("barrier," in Arabic) region, the area of extensive swamps the size of the state of Maine, dividing northern and southern Sudan along the tenth degree latitude, was successfully penetrated for the first time by three Egyptian government expeditions. The steamer and the gun were decisive in subduing the natural forces and the hostile tribes that had withstood for centuries any northern penetration of the region behind the Sudd.

For the next thirty years, no effective administration was established in Southern Sudan. At first the government imposed its monopoly on the region's vast reservoir of ivory, but the Egyptian government was forced by foreign consuls to abandon its monopoly. In 1841 European interests in the Mediterranean forced Mohammed Ali Pasha to abandon his dreams of independence and of carving his own empire from the declining Ottoman Empire. However, he was granted hereditary rule of Egypt and its dependencies. European influences, and especially that of England and France emerged as new and determining factors in Egypt as in the rest of the Ottoman Empire.

By 1834, the number of European consulates in Alexandria had risen to fourteen, including that of the United States. The number of European residents

4

by 1833 was over five thousand, mostly engaged in trade. They enjoyed the privileges stipulated by the Capitulation Regime, which gave European consulates extra-territorial rights in the Ottoman Empire.[2] By 1844, the number had jumped to 6,150. Under the xenophobic Abbas, 1849-1854, three thousand Greeks were ordered to leave the country, most of whom returned under Said Pasha, 1854-1863.

The abandoning of the monopoly of trade in ivory in Southern Sudan in 1848 opened that region to un-harnessed adventurers, the riff-raff of Europe, the Levantine, and Northern Sudan, whose main motive was profit. Violence erupted between them and the Southern Sudanese tribes over trade. The tribesmen were no longer satisfied with colorful beads and cheap cloth, and demanded cattle for their ivory--this, in a region where a man's worth was measured by the number of cattle in his possession. The only possible way for the interlopers to obtain cattle was through the robbing of one tribe to pay another.

Slaves were captured along with cattle. The southern captives fit neatly with the already estab-lished criteria of slavery in the Nile Valley. They were non-Muslims and non-Arabs. Moreover, the accessible southern tribes beyond Bahr al Arab in Bahr al Ghazal had been raided for slaves in the past, and were part of the traditional reservoir of black slaves. This vast region, extending beyond the Sudd to the Lakes region in Central Africa, became the main source of black slaves thereafter. Chiefs of the large tribes collaborated willy-nilly with the motley slave traders, who gradually emerged as overlords with known spheres of influence and organized gangs of armed retainers, mostly from Northern Sudan. For two decades, these overlords penetrated the region, explored it long before the advent of European explorers, and captured slaves.

Thousands of slaves were sent annually up the Nile and the desert routes to Northern Sudan, and from there by land and sea to Egypt and Arabia. Khartoum emerged as one of the most important and notorious commercial centers of Northeast Africa, with the slave trade being the backbone of its commercial activities. Very little was known in the rest of the world about drastic expansion of the slave trade and its atrocities.

* * *

5

Since the 1830's, the British anti-slavery groups
had been applying pressure in varying degree on
Mohammed Ali Pasha to abolish the slave trade in Egypt
and its dependencies. He and his two successors,
Abbas Pasha and Said Pasha, promised to take action,
and occasionally did so half-heartedly; but the slave
trade continued.

In 1842, Mohammed Ali closed the slave market,
wakalat al Jallaba, in Cairo. In 1854, Said Pasha
officially abolished the slave trade and established
a control post at Fashoda in Southern Sudan. Two years
later, he issued a decree to free those slaves who so
wanted, and closed the remaining slave markets in Egypt.
In the same year, he iwsued orders forbidding payment
of officials in Sudan in slaves.

These measures failed to stop the slave trade
because they were never seriously enforced. The Sultan
of Turkey was persuaded to issue a firman in 1857
ordering Said Pasha to take stronger measures against
the slave trade. The failure of the successive viceroys
of Egypt to abolish the slave trade was understandable.
Slavery and the slave trade were so entrenched in the
social and economic structure of the societies of Egypt
and the Sudan that their abolition by decree was
inconceivable. Whatever steps taken were meant to
appease foreign interests and to serve Turco-Egyptian
interests. Despite all the measures taken by Said Pasha
to abolish the slave trade, he formed a personal body-
guard of black slaves specially purchased for that
purpose in 1859.

Moreover, the British government, as distinct from
the humanitarian groups, was lukewarm in its pressures
on the Egyptian government to abolish the slave trade.
The British Consulate in Khartoum was suppressed in
1864 after its vice-consul, John Petherick (1813-1882),
was accused by a Maltese slave trader of being involved
in the traffic himself. Only in the 1870's did the
British government begin to move with resolve and
determination.

The year 1863 was a decisive landmark in the fight
of the British humanitarian circles against the slave
trade in the Nile Valley. In that year, three British
explorers, Samuel White Baker (1821-1893), John Hanning
Speke (1827-1864), and James Augustus Grant (1827-1892),
visited Southern Sudan. They wrote extensively of the
atrocities of the slave trade in the British papers
and the anti-slavery movement's publications. The

information created a great uproar in the humanitarian circles of Great Britain. The British government was forced to increase its pressure on both the Ottoman Empire and its dependencies to bring the abominable traffic in human beings to an end.

Early in 1863, the Emancipation Proclamation had been issued in the United States. The Proclamation was received with relief in Great Britain. The anti-slavery society could thenceforth turn its efforts and energies toward suppressing the slave trade in East and Northeast Africa. The news concerning the rampant slave trade in the Upper Nile could not have come at a better time. Immediately the movement focused its attention and tremendous potential on the Nile Valley.

The death of Said Pasha early in 1863 and the ascendancy of Ismail Pasha (1830-1895) as Viceroy generated new hopes of the possibility of initiating more serious steps to abolish the slave trade in the Nile Valley. Ismail had completed his studies in Vienna and Paris, and was considered to be liberal and amenable to Western ideas and values. Like his grandfather, Mohammed Ali, he was ambitious, aspiring to gain independence from Turkey, to modernize Egypt, and to expand it in East and Central Africa. In 1867 he obtained the conferment of the hereditary title of Khedive on himself and his direct male descendants, thus bringing himself one step closer to independence.

When the Suez Canal was opened in 1869, Egypt gained a new importance as the gateway to Africa and the Far East. As such, Egypt became the backbone of the British imperial global strategy. In 1875 the British government gladly purchased Ismail's holdings in the Suez Canal, which constituted forty percent of its capital. In the same year, the finances of the Egyptian government were placed under an Anglo-French Commission, an action interpreted by Egyptian nationalists as tantamount to loss of whatever sovereignty Egypt possessed. The constant conflicts between Ismail and the Commission led to his deposition in 1879. Three years later, in 1882, British troops occupied Egypt.

It was within the context of these drastic political and economic developments during the previous decade that the British humanitarian efforts to abolish slavery and the slave trade were able to achieve what it had failed to achieve for almost half a century.

7

In 1869 Sir Samuel White Baker was appointed at the suggestion of the Prince of Wales (afterward, King Edward VII), governor of Equatoria. His mission was to expand and consolidate Egyptian administration in the southern region and to suppress the slave trade. Baker scored partial success during his four-year tenure in both objectives. He was met with resistance and hostility by the Egyptian officials, the slave traders and the southern tribes because of his heavy-handedness and overbearing manner.

Baker was followed by another Englishman, Charles George Gordon (1833-1885), who adopted the same two objectives. His demeanor and style were different, however. He befriended the tribes and was met with less hostility by the Turco-Egyptian officials; but his success in suppressing the slave trade was limited. He discovered that slavery and the slave trade were so deeply rooted in the Sudanese society and in the Turco-Egyptian administration, that combating them in one region was not enough to eradicate them.

Gordon was convinced that Turco-Egyptian officials were not trustworthy when it came to abolishing the slave trade because of their involvement in it. He therefore employed eight European subordinates, among them two American officers, Charles Caille-Long (1842-1917), and William P. Campbell (?-1875).

The official Egyptian reaction to these new pressures to abolish the slave trade was meant to mollify foreign pressure rather than to eradicate slavery and the slave trade. For example, Ismail in 1873 ordered his officials to stop the slave trade completely. One year later, a law was published abolishing slavery; and yet in 1877, Ismail dispatched his mother's black eunuch to the Port of Massawa on the Red Sea to obtain hundreds of slaves and eunuchs for the royal ceremonies in Cairo.[3]

To compound the situation, Gordon, a mercurial administrator, appointed as lieutenant-governor of Gondokoro in 1874 Mohammed Abu Saud Bey al Aqqad (?-1881), the infamous Egyptian slave trader in Equatoria who had been arrested and sent in chains to Khartoum by Baker one year earlier. Gordon believed by doing so, that he could both neutralize him, and use his knowledge of the region and his influence on slavers to achieve his own end.

Following the same line of reasoning, the Khedive appointed as governor of Bahr al Ghazal, al Zubair Rahma Mansur (1830-1913), the strongest Northern Sudanese slave trader in that region. Zubair had succeeded by sheer courage and power of personality to become the overlord of the extensive Bahr al Ghazal region. In 1874 he invaded and conquered the kingdom of Darfur, which he aspired to bring under his control. As a result, he clashed with Ismail Ayub (?-1884), the Governor-General, and proceeded to Egypt to complain. In Egypt he was created Pasha, and retained honorably in exile until the reconquest of the Sudan in 1898.

The conciliatory attitude taken toward these two notorious slave traders cast a long shadow of doubt on the sincerity of the Egyptian government in abolishing the slave trade on one hand, and reflected the naivete of Gordon in dealing with the slave traders on the other. Apparently, the government was more concerned with territorial expansion, while Gordon was not enthusiastic about it.

In 1876, Gordon resigned as governor of Equatoria in disgust and frustration, the declining financial situation, combined with the uncontrollable slave trade being the primary causes. In the following year, he was appointed Governor-General of the whole of Sudan, a post he believed, along with the British Anti-Slavery Society, would enable him to clamp down on the sources of supply in the Upper Nile.

In 1877, the Convention for the Suppression of the Slave Trade in Negro and Abyssinian Slaves between Great Britain and Egypt was signed.* Gordon criticized the Convention which he perceived to be an unnecessary obstruction to his own plans. According to one authority:

> Gordon held the view that the Khedive
> was forced by Britain to sign the
> slave treaty and that the provisions
> of the treaty were beyond the powers
> of the Khedive to carry out vigorously
> in the outlying provinces of Egypt.
> Until the beginning of 1881, Gordon
> continued to criticize the Convention
> as impracticable. He held that the
> Convention stipulated the liberation
> of slaves without compensating their
> owners and that this would impoverish

* See Appendix B

the latter and thereby cause a
great loss of revenue to the Sudan
and Cairo Exchequer.[4]

Nevertheless, Gordon was forced to embark on a
ruthless campaign against the slave trade in 1878,
spurred on by the criticism of his foot-dragging by
the British Anti-Slavery Society, as well as by the
imminent removal from power of his friend, Khedive
Ismail. Convinced that he would not serve under
another Khedive, Gordon acted quickly so as to be
remembered as the man who had suppressed the slave
trade. Assisted by his over-zealous subordinates, the
Italian, Romolo Gessi (1831-1881), and Sicilian Jew,
Edward Carl Oscar Theodore Schnitzer, known as Emin
Pasha (1840-1892), he started an all-out war against
the slave trade. Firing most of his Egyptian subordinates, Gordon appointed fourteen Europeans to replace
them. In doing so, he confirmed the already existing
conceptions that the drive to abolish slavery and the
slave trade was a Christian plot to undermine and
discredit Islam.

The Northern Sudanese slave traders were scrupu-
lously rooted out of their strongholds in Equatoria and
Bahr al Ghazal, while the green light was given to
their traditional adversaries, the nomads of Kordofan
and Darfur, to hunt them down. They gladly obliged.

Dispossessed and hunted, the slave traders began
to rally around the embittered Sulaiman, the son of al
Zubair Pasha, the slave trader exiled in Cairo.
Dismissed from his post as vice-governor of the Bahr al
Ghazal, a position to which Gordon had appointed him,
Sulaiman led the slave traders' rebellion. The energetic Gessi led the government troops and defeated him.
Sulaiman and several of his lieutenants were hanged in
1879. Thus, a severe blow was dealt the slave traders
in the Sudan. Political discontent was coupled with
economic hardship, resentment of the Turco-Egyptian
corruption, and memories of its earlier brutal reprisals.
The outbreak of the Mahdi Revolution in 1881 was
welcomed by the Sudanese.

Gordon, who had resigned as Governor-General in
1879 after the desposition of Ismail, was recalled in
1884 to evacuate the Egyptian garrisons from the Sudan.
Upon his arrival in Berber, he declared the 1877
Convention null and void, and informed the Sudanese
that they could own as many slaves as they wished,
thus contradicting his position of six years ago.

10

He offered to appoint the Mahdi as King of Kordofan.
Both his declaration and his offer missed the point,
however, and were treated with indifference and contempt. Like many of his countemporaries, Gordon had
misunderstood the Mahdist revolution and its fundamentalist revolutionary nature. When the Mahdists stormed
Khartoum early in 1885, Gordon paid with his life the
price of his miscalculation, contradictions, and
stubbornness.

Between 1885 and 1898, the Mahdist state ruled the
Sudan. The slave trade became a government monopoly,
and only a small proportion of slaves were exported to
Arabia; and few still were smuggled into Egypt.

Another Convention, more comprehensive and free
of the loopholes of the earlier convention, was signed
in 1895 between Great Britain and Egypt. Slavery and
the slave trade in white, brown and black was prohibited.* The new Convention had two main objectives:
to abolish slavery, and to help the freed slaves in
their new life. The infringement on their individual
freedom became a serious crime.

The occupation of the Sudan in 1898 by the Anglo-
Egyptian troops brought the Mahdist State to an end.
Article XI of the Condominium Agreement for the
Administration of the Sudan between Great Britain and
Egypt in 1899 reads:

> The importation of slaves into the
> Sudan, as also their exportation,
> is absolutely prohibited. Provision
> shall be made by Proclamation for
> the enforcement of this Regulation.

Except for a few isolated incidents, the Nile
Valley in general, and the Sudan in particular, stepped
into the twentieth century free of slavery and the
slave trade for the first time in recorded history.
Such a revolutionary step was the outcome of changing
social and political circumstances and the efforts of
British officials and humanitarians.

* * *

The number of slaves traded in the nineteenth
century is very difficult to produce. No records were

* See Appendix C

11

kept by the traders or government officials. The trade in white slaves was conducted in secret, the concubines secluded behind the harems' walls. Whatever numbers we have are estimates given by European travellers and over-zealous supporters of the anti-slavery movement.

The average number of black slaves in Egypt at any time during the nineteenth century was estimated at between twenty-five and thirty thousand, or one percent of the Egyptian population. The high mortality rate, especially during recurrent epidemics, such as cholera and smallpox, and the low reproductivity among the slaves were responsible for a fifty percent death rate among them. This resulted in the need of importation of 12,500 to 15,000 annually to replenish the black slave population. The four Manumission Bureaus in Egypt freed more than 8,092 slaves, who sought their freedom papers between 1877 and 1882.[5]

As to the number of slaves in Northern Sudan, or those killed during hunting raids, no reliable esti-mates are available. No doubt the difficulty in identifying black slaves in Northern Sudan from the rest of the population was responsible for this lack. However, one-half of the population of Khartoum and Shendi were believed to be slaves. One would assume that other urban centers, such as al Obeid, which were also thriving slave-trading centers, would have the same percentage. Gordon, in one of his wild guesses, estimated that seven-eighths of the Sudanese population were slaves.

The prices of slaves in the nineteenth century constituted another problem. Travellers quoted different currencies which are difficult to translate into today's fluctuating currencies.

The status of the members of the elite class in both Egypt and Northern Sudan was measured by the number of slaves they owned. Paradoxically, most of those elites were the offspring of concubines. Although the majority of the concubines were white, some were not. Caliph al Mustansir (1036-1094) was the son of such a black concubine. Most travellers to Egypt agreed that the lot of the slaves was better than that of the free, poor tillers of land, the fellaheen, the religious minorities, and women. They were also in agreement as to the better treatment of slaves in the Islamic world as compared tc that in the Western world.

* * *

The position of Islam regarding slavery was clear
from the beginning. A few of the early converts to
Islam were black slaves. The majority of converts
were free and several among them were from the leading
families of the Quraish tribe. Both the Koran and the
Prophet's tradition sanctioned slavery, but emphatically
encouraged the good treatment of slaves. Manumission
of slaves was recommended repeatedly as a work of piety.
The absolution of certain excesses was attainable and
their kind treatment in general were urged.

This lenient attitude of Islam toward slaves was
enforced by its polygamous nature. A Muslim was allowed
to have four wives, if he could treat them justly and
with even-handedness. He was also allowed innumerable
concubines. The male offspring of such liaisons were
customarily recognized in most cases, especially if
they had distinguished themselves in some way. Slaves
were also accorded clear-cut rights.

There is no racial prejudice in the Koran. The
much-quoted section from Chapter XLIX, Verse Thirteen
reads:

> O people! We have created you from
> a male and a female and we have made
> you into confederacies and tribes so
> that you may come to know one another.
> The noblest among you in the eyes of
> God is the most pious, for God is
> omniscient and well-informed.

Prophet Mohammed was reported to have elaborated on the
same theme of human equality. But the expansion of the
Islamic Empire in Africa and Asia created race con-
sciousness and superiority among the conquerors.
However, no "apartheid" system as that which developed
in the United States did so in the Islamic world. The
concept of Umma, the community of Islam, served to
continuously erode racial prejudice.

Yet slavery in blacks lingered in some parts of
the Islamic world deep into the twentieth century. No
movement to abolish slavery developed in the Islamic
world. The dichotomy which sanctioned slavery on one
hand, while urging lenience and manumission on the
other, was responsible for the absence of any abolition
movement, as well as the advocacy of the continuation
of slavery.

13

Slave revolts abound in the history of Islam, the most famous being the Zanj (Negro) revolt in Iraq in A.D. 869-883. Black soldiers in the Nile valley also instigated several revolts that forced the ruling elite to reach compromises with them. One such revolt occurred in Kassala, Sudan as late as 1865.

The European economic and political expansion in the nineteenth century paved the way for the attack by humanitarians on the two institutions of slavery and the slave trade. To the ruling elites in the Nile Valley--politicians and Ulamma, doctors of Islamic Shari'a (law), this was considered an unwarranted interference. Even the ordinary people shared this position. Some went so far as to trace it back to a lingering Crusader spirit in the West.

All during the nineteenth century, Egypt was ruled by a secular Turkish element, as well as by a native, spiritual and non-official religious class from al Azhar University. The latter group was nationalistic, against the Turkish elites as well as the Europeans. This fact was responsible to a great extent for the failure of the pressure on the secular officials and the steps they had reluctantly taken to eradicate slavery and the slave trade.

In Tunisia, the declaration of emancipating slaves was easily enacted after 1846 by the French because of the collaboration of secular and spiritual leaders. Although slavery was declared by the two leading religious leaders of Tunis, Hanafi and Maliki, as lawful in principle, it was considered by them as "regrettable in consequences. Of the three considerations particularized, two are of religious nature, the third political (maslaha syasiyya)."[6]

In other words, it was considered expedient by these religious authorities for the Bey of Tunis to comply with the French in abolishing slavery and the slave trade. When Mohammed Ali was approached by the British Consul to take similar steps, the Pasha replied that the Bey of Tunis had acted hastily and without reflection; but that it was a dangerous example for him to emulate.[7]

The leading Egyptian Islamic reformer, Mohammed Abdu, in exile after 1882, argued that the abolition of slavery was in accordance with the spirit of Islam. The Koran and the Prophet's tradition, like the Bible,

14

lent themselves to such an interpretation. Abdu's argument was presented to the British Anti-Slavery Society in defense of Islam. As such, it was a reaction for argument's sake rather than an initiative that could have affected the course of events in the Nile Valley had it been declared by him earlier. Evidently Abdu and his colleagues were religious reformers and nationalists rather than humanitarians in the Western sense of the word.

In 1891 another Egyptian scholar, Ahmed Chafik argued that slavery was tolerated by Islam in its early days as a "temporary necessity," while the purpose was to abolish it eventually.[8]

It is interesting to note that the two major upheavals in the Nile Valley in 1881 had not aimed at abolishing slavery and the slave trade. The Mahdist revolution in the Sudan was mainly a fundamentalist Islamic revolt aimed at eradicating corruption, and restoration of the purity of Islam and its spread throughout the Islamic world. Ahmed Arabi's military uprising in Egypt was primarily a nationalistic movement aimed against foreign domination of Egypt. Both upheavals were eventually suppressed by the British military might, 'Arabi's in 1882 and the Mahdia in 1898. It was only after British political domination of both countries that slavery and the slave trade were finally eradicated in the Nile Valley. However, it should be pointed out that their eradication was not the predominant British motive for the occupation of either Egypt or the Sudan.

Modern writers differ in their assessment of the British efforts to abolish slavery and the slave trade in the Nile Valley. Egyptian historians regard them as Machiavellian, more intended to rob Egypt of its rightful possessions in Central Africa. British historians consider them proudly as the best thing that ever happened to the body and soul of the Nile Valley. Some Northern Sudanese historians consider the British efforts as unwarranted interference that hindered the natural twin processes of islamization and arabization, and paved the way for hatred and aberration between Northerners and Southerners. The Southern Sudanese scholars agree with the British, adding that had it not been for British interference, their people would have been annihilated. Interestingly enough, there is a grain of truth in each of the four arguments.

PART ONE:

PUBLIC REACTIONS

Chapter I

THE INVISIBLE CONNECTION: THE HAMITIC MYTH

By the end of the eighteenth century, the Bible was still supreme as the primary source of historical information and moral guidance in the Western world. In the United States, where Bible-reading groups were popular and widespread, the holy, generalized pronouncements of the Bible were frequently invoked by the rank and file of the dominant white Christian settlers and frontiersmen to justify or condemn the ondoging systematic extermination of native Americans and the perpetuation of the enslavement of Africans.   The American genius of reconciling idealism and a nascent exploitative racist capitalism was already in the ascendancy.   The rest of the world was viewed by these settlers through their own socioeconomic philosophy and their interpretations of the biblical historical outlook.

Due to geography and distance, the Nile Valley, unlike the rest of Africa, was not a known source of African slaves to the New World.   Nor was it a partner in any significant way to the New World's letitimate commerce.   Yet, historically and intellectually, it was an integral part of the Judeo-Christian heritage.   Its proximity to the Holy Land involved it, directly or indirectly, in the historical developments of the region and faith.   On balance, Egypt had figured rather unpleasantly in the Bible.   The decisive role it played as an emerging Muslim state in finally expelling the Christian crusaders from the Holy Land and especially Jerusalem in the thirteenth century, had not particularly endeared her to the Christian world.

The occupation of Egypt in 1798 by Napolean Bonaparte was the historical catalyst that turned upside-down the existing Western classification of races and interpretation of the biblical historical account.   The need for substitutes and/or adaptation became urgent.   The discovery, by one of Napoleon's soldiers, of the Rosetta Stone, a slab inscribed with a decree in both Greek and hieroglyphics honoring the successor of Alexander the Great in Egypt, and the subsequent deciphering of the hieroglyphics by the French scholar, Jean-Francois Champollion, in 1822 led

to the birth of Egyptology. The brilliant achievements
of the ancient civilizations of the Nile Valley began
gradually to unfold, through amateur and professional
research, before an incredulous West. Until then,
these civilizations were only partially known to a few
Western scholars through the writings of classical
historians and geographers such as Herodotus, Strabo,
and Sexus Julius Africanus.

Before the rise of Egyptology, the Greek and Roman
empires were considered by far the most ancient and
brilliant civilizations of antiquity. The discovery
of the ancient civilizations of the Nile Valley blew
both myths to shreds. They had not only preceded the
two European civilizations- but had contributed in no
mean way to their intellectual and cultural growth.
The fact that the Nile Valley was part of Africa and
inhabited by mulattoes and blacks, as it was believed
at the time; plus the timing of the revelation of its
glorious past, when the supremacy of the white man
was taken for granted, made it impossible for the West
to accept such revelations without contradicting its
existing value system.

The American public and scholarly interest in the
Nile Valley civilizations was, from the start, marked
by intense emotional reaction. The United States was
a slave society in disarray, plagued by the post-Revo-
lution conflicts between anti-slavery and pro-slavery
groups, and between the religious monogenists, who
believed in the unity of the origin of mankind, and
their secular opponents, the polygenists, who believed
in the multiplicity of human origin and considered the
Negro a subhuman. These conflicts were not just
academic or moral, as they were in Europe. They were
real and had a serious impact on the very foundations
of the American society.

Even before the discovery of the ancient Nile
Valley civilizations, the mixture of races in Egypt
was unsettling to a society that was already polarized
over the questions of race and slavery. A politician
opposed to the emancipation of slaves said in 1806:

> I presume...that no white man shall
> look forward with any complacency to
> that condition of society, in which
> the two races will be blended
> together, when the distinction of

20

color shall be obliterated: when,
like the Egyptians, we shall exhibit
a dual and uniform complexion.[1]

When the ancient civilization of Egypt was
discovered, the very basis of the cosmology of white
America was shattered. It was based mainly, as far
as the question of slavery and the Negro race were
concerned, on the curse of Noah and his youngest son,
Ham, as related in the Book of Genesis:

Cursed by Canaan
A servant of servants shall he be
unto his brethren

Later interpretations in the Babylonian Talmud,
a collection of oral tradition of the Jews, which
appeared in the sixth century, extended the curse from
servitude to blackness. The rise of the African slave
trade across the Red Sea and the Mediterranean during
medieval times by the Muslim Arabs as slave hunters
and merchants, and the Jews as middlemen across the
Mediterranean provided the contemporary interpreters
of the Talmud with the motivation needed to weave an
elaborate Hamitic myth. Noah's curse emerged as:

Now I cannot beget the fourth son
whose children I would have ordered
to serve you and your brothers.
Therefore it must be Canaan, your
first-born, whom they enslave. And
you have disabled me...doing things
in blackness of night, Canaan's
children shall be ugly and black.
Moreover, because you twisted your
head around to see my nakedness,
your grandchildren's hair shall be
twisted in kinks, and their eyes
red; again because your lips jested
at my misfortune, theirs shall
swell; and because you neglected
my nakedness, they shall go naked,
and their male members shall be
shamefully elongated.[2]

The trans-Atlantic slave trade in the sixteenth
century and afterward overshadowed the Muslim slave
trade while inheriting and expanding its attitudes
toward black African slaves. To the West, the Judeo-

Christian heritage concerning Ham's descendants'
enslavement and their color came in handy. Although
American slavery had reduced the black slave to a
chattel and surpassed other slave systems in its
cruelty, it was by no means the forerunner in identifying slavery with black Africa. The groundwork for
such identification had been already laid elsewhere.
The Americans inherited it, elaborated on it, and turned
it into a concrete social and legal structure.

The anti-slavery groups and the free black
community welcomed the discovery of the Nile Valley
civilizations, and utilized it extensively in their
arguments about the African Negro's contribution to
civilization and his right to be emancipated. Their
arguments were aimed at the very foundation of the
existing status quo. It became evident that the curse
of Ham and its subsequent interpretations had backfired
and every new discovery in the field of Egyptology was
a further condemnation of it.

As early as the 1830's, the American general public
was beginning to show a deep interest in the Nile
Valley civilizations. George Gliddon, the first
consular agent of the United States in Cairo, and a
pioneering student of ancient Egyptian history, was
touring the United States lecturing on ancient Egypt
and exhibiting his numerous artifacts. It was reported
that some of his lectures were attended by an audience
of more than two thousand, while his booklet, "Ancient
Egypt: Her Monuments, Hierglyphics, History and
Archaeology," sold more than 20,000 in its first
edition, for the price of twenty-five cents.[3]

One reason for the popularity of Gliddon's lectures
and books was his theme, which his all-white audience
found particularly appealing and comforting at the time.
He was direct, unsophisticated, and to the point:

> It has been shown that there was a
> curse on Ham, or on Mizraim. We
> know that the curse on Canaan
> affected him morally, and not
> physically. We have seen that Shem,
> Ham and Japheth, were of one blood
> as brothers. We know that Shem and
> Ham were twin brothers. We know
> that Shem, the parent of Semitic
> nations, and Japhet, the parent of

Circassian tribes, were Caucasians.
It follows therefore, that Ham was
Caucasian also, and so were all his
children, and Mizraim in particular,
when he entered Egypt.[4]

The Egyptians, the sons of Mizraim, were thus
rehabilitated by Gliddon from their previous designation
as black slaves by reason of the curse of Noah on his
son, Ham.

The "negroid" presence in Egypt was simply dismissed by Gliddon as the result of the intermarriage and
mixture between the Caucasian Egyptians and their black
slaves from the south--an explanation that strengthened
his audiences' racial prejudices and lulled their fears.
Famous American universities and scholars came to the
rescue, too. According to the historian Edith Sanders:

Perhaps because slavery was both
still legal and profitable in the
United States, and because it was
deemed necessary and right to
protect it, there arose an American
school of anthropology which attempted
to prove scientifically that the
Egyptian was a caucasian, far
removed from the inferior Negro.
As Mannheim said, each intellectual
stand is functionally dependent on
the differentiated social group
reality standing behind it. Such
workers as Dr. Morton, assisted
in various ways by Josiah Nott and
George Gliddon, collected, measured,
interpreted and described the human
crania. The comparative studies
made of crania led Morton to
believe that the Egyptian osteo-
logical formation was Caucasian,
and that it was a race indigenous
to the Nile Valley.[5]

At the same time as the forces of white supremacy
were propagating their newly updated Hamitic theory in
the United States and elsewhere, a black scholar,
James W.C. Pennington, published a booklet approaching
the subject of Noah's curse from a new angle. His
purpose was, according to him, to present "a collocation

23

of historical facts so arranged as to present a just view of our (black) origin."[6] Using the same passages from the Book of Genesis that Gliddon and his associates had used, he argued that the Ethiopians were not the descendants of Canaan. Sarcastically, he asked those who were invoking Noah's curse to justify the enslavement of the Africans to set them free and to "compensate them for false-enslavement, and go get the Canaanites."[7] More seriously, he argued that the Egyptians were the children of Mizraim, and the Ethiopians, the children of Cush. According to him they were not only cousins, but

> ...confederated in the same govern-
> ment, and soon became the same
> people in politics, literature, and
> peculiarities. As evidence of this
> down to the time of Herodotus,
> eighteen of the three hundred
> Egyptian sovereigns were Ethiopians.[8]

After the trauma of the Civil War, the emotional intensity of white America concerning the origin of the Egyptian civilization subsided, for obvious reasons. White America, however, continued to cling to its belief that the ancient Egyptians were Caucasian. For the emancipated blacks, the question remained highly emotional. The anti-slavery societies having disintegrated, and their white members having gone their separate ways, the emancipated blacks were left to face overt and covert racism on their own. In many ways, the identity crisis of black America was worse under the banner of freedom than it had been during slavery. It was further complicated by the wide publicity given in the West to the "Muslim Arab" slave trade in black Africans in the Nile Valley.

The anti-slavery movement in Great Britain, after the demise of the trans-Atlantic slave trade, had become engaged full-time in combating the slave trade in the Nile Valley and East Africa, which had reached its peak in the 1860's. Psychologically, the black American theologians and scholars found it increasingly difficult to identify with the Egyptians, continuously referred to as the perpetrators of the slave trade in Sudan. The fact that more discoveries were made in Nubia and Sudan proper helped those black Americans to shift their emphasis to these new regions, beyond the First Cataract, where the civilization of black

Kush had flourished in the eighth century B.C. They argued that the Kushites were the ones who had laid the foundation of civilization in Egypt. The blackness of some of the descendants of Ham was accepted, while the curse of Noah was dismissed irreverently as the ravings of a drunken old man.

Said a leading black scholar, Rufus L. Perry:

> It is indisputable that some of the descendants of Noah were known as black people, even in the earliest ages. Biblical scholars tell us, that the etymological signification of the word Ham is, swarthy; and that Ethiopian, the name applied to a descendant of the swarthy Ham by the Greeks, means black, burnt. So much for the color of the ancient ancestry of the modern Negro....

> The hair and the color distinguish the different species. Now, in hair and color, the ancient inhabitants of the Nile and the Niger, who gave civilization to both Greece and Rome, were the exact type of the modern Ethiopians; the ancient differ only in this, that they represented a great civilization.... Those who see no connection between the degraded modern African and the noble ancient Cushite or Ethiopian, forget that for centuries the Negro has suffered from the cupidity of other races, from the "league with death and the covenant with hell" into which his white brother entered against him. It does seem to be clear that the present condition of the Negro is the direct result of climate, and more especially of slavery and the slave trade.[9]

The rather amateurish American perceptions and interpretations by both blacks and whites of the ancient Nile Valley civilizations that had preceded the American academic professional contribution at the turn of the century constitute a unique and revealing

soul-searching exercise of a Western slave society--
including masters, slaves and their offspring--
attempting to break away from an inescapable heritage
by reaching out to a remote past in the ancient world.

Even now, more than one century later, the question
of the origin of the ancient Egyptians, who laid the
foundation of that great civilization, remains an
emotional and basic issue for militant black historians.

Although the development of the Hamitic myth in
the twentieth century is not within the scope of this
study, it is important to point out that the mere
existence of such a development is indicative of the
fact that the wounds, prejudices, and attitudes of a
slave society outlive the abolition of slavery--a
simple historical and sociological truism proved by
the recent history of the two slave societies of the
United States and the Nile Valley. Racism born of
slavery dies hard.

Chapter II

AMERICAN TRAVELERS TO THE NILE VALLEY:
IMPRESSIONS AND CONCEPTIONS

In the period between 1823 and 1841, Egypt was
visited by about sixty American tourists; and except
for the Civil War years, their numbers gradually
increased until they reached four thousand annually in
the 1880's, when a visit to Egypt became a fad among
the well-to-do.[1] Several of them published their
impressions and reminiscences in monographs, at a time
when the Western world was discovering anew the achievements of the Nile Valley's ancient civilizations.
Their books dealing with contemporary Egypt and Sudan
must have directly or indirectly shaped and affected
the American attitudes and opinions about the Nile
Valley and its peoples.

American writings about the Nile Valley in the
nineteenth century lend themselves to be divided into
two periods: those written before the Emancipation
Proclamation of January 1863; and those written after
the Civil War, when slavery became illegal and non-
existent throughout the United States. They could also
be further divided into those written by tourists who
visited Egypt where white concubines from Eastern
Europe, brown Abyssinians from Ethiopia, and black
slaves from Western and Southern Sudan were imported;
and those who visited the Sudan from which the black
slaves were captured and purchased for domestic use
in Northern Sudan, or exported to Egypt and across the
Red Sea to Arabia and the rest of the Ottoman Empire.
The latter group of tourists who penetrated the desert
to the Sudan was smaller, more aggressive and knowl-
edgeable about the region, and had a specific purpose
in mind. The hardships and risks of the journey were
not for the ordinary tourists searching for pleasure,
sightseeing, and a mild, sunny and dry winter.

Except for an obscure "colored man" called John
Johnson, who died in Alexandria in 1864, and Frederick
Douglass and his wife, who visited Egypt in 1887, all
the American tourists who visited the Nile Valley in
the nineteenth century were white.

27

PRE-CIVIL WAR TRAVELERS: I. EGYPT

According to available information, the first American to visit Egypt was John Ledyard, who had accompanied Captain Cook (1727-1779) on his famous trip around the world. Ledyard was ordered out of Russia by Empress Catherine for misconduct; and was later employed by the British Association for Promoting the Discovery of the Interior of Africa. He left London in June of 1788 for Egypt. His plan, "to travel southwest, about three hundred leagues west, to a black king," was unfulfilled because of his death in Cairo.[2]

In 1820 two American mercenaries joined the Egyptian army in preparation for the invasion of the Sudan. Both embraced Islam and assumed Muslim names. The first was George Bathune English, known as Mohammed Effendi, and the second was known only by his Muslim name, Khalil Agha.[3]

English wrote a book about the Turco-Egyptian campaign entitled, <u>A Narrative of the Expedition to Dongola and Sennar</u> (1822), considered to be the first written on the subject in any European language. He claimed that he was appointed by Mohammed Ali Pasha, the Viceroy of Egypt, as commander of the artillery. Because of an eye ailment, however, English was unable to play a significant role in the conquest, so that his main contribution was his memoirs.

In his introduction, English wrote that the main purpose behind Mohammed Ali's conquest of the Sudan was to resume commercial relations between the two countries after they were served as a result of the political chaos caused by the domination of the Sha'iquiya tribe of the region, and the attacks of its armed bands on merchant caravans.[4] The main items of trade from the Sudan were black slaves who were in demand in Egypt and Turkey. His interpretation of the purpose of the conquest was contradicted by Mohammed Bey Khusraw the Daftardar, who conquered Kordofan, which were quite explicit as to the main purpose: "...the end of all troubles and this expense is to procure negroes. Please show zeal in carrying out our wishes in this capital matter."[5]

English described in detail the first-hunting expedition sent by Ismail Pasha after the fall of Sennar and Kordofan to fulfill his father's wish. The expedition attacked "the mountains of Bakki, on the southern fringes of Sennar, inhabited by the Pagans... (who) found that spear and swords...were not a match to fire arms."[6]

After the natives' defeat, the expedition returned with all the inhabitants, mostly women and children. English described the prisoners as resembling "the savages of America; they were almost covered with beads and trinkets, made of pebbles, bones and ivory."[7] He failed to display any emotion or express any comdemnation of the conquest of the Sudan or the enslavement of the "pagan" people. To him, a recent convert to Islam, they were "pagans" who resembled the savages of America; and that justified their enslavement.

English estimated the population of the town of Shendi, a commercial center in Northern Sudan, as being between five and six thousand, half of whom were slaves from Abyssinia and the Nuba mountains. He described their prices as being reasonable. A pretty Abyssinian girl was sold for fifty dollars.[8]

Another American traveler who visited Egypt was a Reverend Michael Russell who, in his book published in 1831, attributed the origins of the ancient Nile Valley civilizations to Asians who had come in search of fertile lands, commerce and gold, bringing with them civilization, science, and the liberal arts. Like most foreign travelers before and after him, he visited the slave market in Cairo, and was particularly attracted to the Abyssinian female slaves:

> The Ethiopian women brought to
> Egypt for sale, though black,
> are exceedingly beautiful; their
> features being perfectly regular,
> and their eyes full of fire. A
> great number of them have been
> purchased by the French during
> their stay in the country.[9]

White Americans such as Rev. Russell, as well as the French, preferred Ethiopian women, whose features were closer to those of the European, than the pure African. It was believed by them that in such women was combined the beauty of the white with the sexuality of the black.[10] Mulatto females were also preferred in the United States at the time for the same reason.

Interestingly enough, Rev. Russell was repulsed by the white female slaves.

> The Circassians at all time are
> exposed for sale in particular markets
> or Khans, and occasionally bring
> large sums of money to the owners.
> Their beauty, however, is not very
> highly prized by Europeans who are
> at a loss to account for those
> lofty descriptions which fill the
> pages of oriental romance, and
> ascribe all the attractions of
> female form to the natives of one
> favored portion of Asia.[11]

The writer, a religious man, did not express any condemnation of the institution of slavery, and it is quite evident that he considered it normal.

George Jones, U.S. Navy chaplain and author, also visited Egypt in the 1830's. He visited the slave market of Cairo and described the female black slaves' hair as being worked up into long ringlets, which fell on either side of the head, and whos cheeks were in some instances marked by scars in regular figures. He believed that the scars were evidently designed to be an addition to their charms.[12]

His observations are interesting because the hairstyle and facial scars to which he referred were popular in Northern Sudan among Muslim rivrain and Arabized tribes. Although slaves were known to have been captured from the non-Muslim tribes of the Nuba mountains and Bahr al-Ghazal, it was not general practice to obtain them from the Muslim rivrain tribes. The only plausible explanation would be that these tribes occasionally dispensed with some of their female slaves who had been raised among them when in need of cash.

Chaplain Jones reported that while they were visiting the slave market, some of the female slaves put on their best looks, inviting them to become their purchasers..."to which, I believe, we felt not the least inclined, though their price was extremely low."[13] He also visited the "madhouse" in Cairo, another tourist attraction, and found the sight of its inmates so mortifying that he sympathized with them,

30

a sympathy not extended to the slaves whose position he apparently accepted.[14]

In 1839 the American traveler, James E. Cooley, journeyed to Egypt, Arabia, and the Holy Land. After visiting the slave market in Cairo, he remarked:

> Here we saw a man in a state of ignorance, degradation, and misery, but little removed from the mere animal or brute creation. It would be impossible to exhibit more deplorable specimens of our species than we saw in that sink of filth, disease and death. There were slaves (mostly from Nubia, Abyssinia, and Dongola) in all the stalls, or in groups, sitting upon the ground or on the balcony. Some were handsome figures, and compactly built; though by far the greater number were ugly, deformed and diseased.[15]

A preceeding reference in his book to the persecuted Jewish minority was more sympathetic. He described them as being tributary to the government, and often in a state of literal slavery.[16]

The slave market became such a tourist attraction that guided tours were organized. The Cairo slave market was a large building divided into upper and lower chambers. The more valuable slaves such as the white females and the eunuchs were relegated to the upper chambers where they were seldom sold or shown to Europeans, and could not be viewed by the general public. Mohammed Ali closed the slave markets in 1842, but selling in different quarters continued in Cairo. Even after slavery was legally prohibited later in the century, tourist agencies continued to organize tours which simulated slave markets in order to satisfy their curious Western customers.[17] Says Cooley, "We soon satisfied our curiosity in the slave market; and taking a turn through the Turkish bazaar, went out at the "Gate of Victory" to view the tombs of the Mamlooks."[18]

The following remarks of Cooley concerning the Circassian and Georgian female slaves were based, according to him, mainly on hearsay and earlier writings:

31

> The Circassian slaves of both sexes
> have never been held in the highest
> estimation of any but the Turks.
> The Abazans stand next in favour with
> them; the Mongrelians next; after
> them the Georgians, then Russians
> and Poles; next the Hungarians and
> Germans, then the Negroes; and last
> of all the Spaniard, Maltese, and
> Franks, whom they despise as drunkards,
> debauchees, idle and mutinous.[19]

Like Rev. Russell before him, Cooley directed his
repulsion and outrage not toward the institution of
slavery, but rather toward those enslaved, black and
white, projecting them as different, less human, and
therefore worthy of bondage.

The dean of American travelers, John Lloyd
Stephens, who visited Egypt in the 1830's, represented
a new class of tourist. His wide travels and famil-
iarity with the various arguments of anti-slavery groups
and their opponents give his remarks about slavery in
the Nile Valley depth and forcefulness which are absent
in earlier writings. Stephens, confronted by the
realities of slavery and the slave trade in the Nile
Valley, was forced to compare them with the American
system. In the process, he expressed intimate thoughts
and attitudes about the issues of slavery and race.
The collision of the two slave societies in the sub-
conscious mind shook off all pretenses and exposed the
naked truth. Upon seeing Sudanese slaves at Jidda
in Saudi Arabia, Stephens said in a rare moment of
truth:

> Among them was every variety of face
> and complexion, and it was at once
> startling and painful to note the
> gradations of man descending to the
> brute. I could almost see the very
> line of separation. Though made in
> God's image, there seemed no ray of
> divinity within them. They did not
> move upon all-fours, it is true, but
> they sat...precisely as we see
> monkeys, baboons, and apes; and as,
> while looking at these miserable
> caricatures of our race, I have some-
> times been almost electrified by a

transient gleam of resemblance
to humanity, so here I was struck
with the closeness of man's
approach to the inferior grade
of animal existence....To such as
these, slavery to the Turk is not
a bitter draught....What is liberty
to men dying for bread, and what
hardship is there in being separated
from parents who have sold them,
or doomed to labor where that labor
is light compared with what they
must endure at home?[20]

Stephen Olin, clergyman and president of Wesleyan
University, 1842-1851, visited Egypt in 1843, and
published two volumes about his travels. He showed a
keen eye for distinguishing the different shades of
color among the population of Egypt, describing the
Egyptians themselves as similar in their complexion to
the American light-colored mulattoes, who were more
"intellectual than the European races." The Nubian
slaves from Northern Sudan were similar, according to
him, to the American dark mulatto, but "still they
were no negroes." He described the slaves from Central
Africa as the real savages: "...the blackest of their
race, with all its peculiarities....They are certainly
more intellectual and sprightly in appearance than our
Africans, free or slaves."

These remarks are interesting in light of the fact
that Rev. Olin, a Yankee, and a slaveholder while
assigned to a Virginia synod, was later selected to
find a basis of agreement for the pro-slavery and anti-
slavery factions within the divided Methodist Episcopal
church. It is reported that Rev. Olin, at the General
Conference of 1844, delivered a speech which gave a
just estimate and full comprehension of the subject of
slavery. One can wonder how such was possible when
Olin obviously had a biased opinion of the black
American population.

Continuing with his description of the Egyptian
population, he found the Copts, the descendants of the
ancient Egyptians, to be a little fairer than the
majority of Egyptians. He attributed that to their
nutritious food and indoor employment. Olin looked
down on their version of Christianity, and accused some
of their priests of running centers for castration of
Negro slave boys.

33

Giving his American readers one of the early glimpses of that abominable practice, Olin wrote that the two towns of Asyut and Girgeh, both predominantly Coptic, furnished Egypt with eunuchs; and that the chief victims were boys from six to eight years of age, purchased by slave-dealers in Sennar and other countries on the Upper Nile, and brought down by caravans to Egypt. There they were sold to the operators at from 1200 to 2500 piasters each. Although a large proportion died as a result of the operation to which they were subjected; nevertheless, the trade was still lucrative in Egypt and Turkey. He estimated that about three hundred eunuchs were sold annually; and that they were seen frequently in Cairo and other parts of Egypt, easily recognizable by their beardless, shriveled faces and feminine voices.[21]

Edward Joy Morris, appointed Minister to Turkey by Lincoln, and who visited Egypt in 1847, provides us with an interesting piece of information in regard to the purchase of slaves by foreigners. Europeans were not prohibited in Egypt from purchasing slaves as they were in Constantinople. Morris relates the story of a "friend" who offered a price equal to eighty dollars for an Abyssinian girl, who refused after the bargain was concluded to "be sold to a Frank, so the bargain was broken up."[22] Apparently, this was a relatively new development, because John Ledyard, the first known American traveler to Egypt (1788) complained of prejudice against Christians, who were forbidden from purchasing slaves, and were not even allowed in the slave market.[23]

It had been reported elsewhere that the French soldiers of Napoleon's army had indeed purchased Ethiopian girls in Egypt and had taken them back to France. Since slavery was still legal in some parts of the United States at the time, it is fairly reasonable to assume that the alleged "friend" was the writer himself or another American. Such an incident poses an important question: Had any slaves, Circassian, Negro, or Ethiopian found their way to the United States from the Nile Valley? If so, then the Nile Valley contributed its symbolic share to the slave population of the New World.

PRE-CIVIL WAR TRAVELERS: II. SUDAN

The American diplomat and poet, Bayard Taylor visited the Sudan in 1852. He provides our second glimpse, after George Bathune English, into that region through American eyes. His book, Journey to Central Africa (1854), contains valuable information about the city of Khartoum, the capital of the Sudan, three decades after its founding, in that critical period of its development as one of the most notorious slave trade centers in the interior of Northeast Africa.

Taylor was a unique traveler who declared from the start that he was not penetrating into the heart of Africa in search of historical and geographical information like other travelers, but to "participate in their free, vigorous, semi-barbaric life."[24] His monograph is replete with sensuous descriptions of the beauty and physical attraction of both sexes in Northern Sudan. We should not overlook, however, the relationship between the writer's literary interest, the purpose behind his penetration into Central America, and the romantic literary movement of the 19th century. That movement's obsession with freedom led some of its followers to glorify the "primitive" life of the "noble savage tribes."

Taylor differed from the typical American traveler. He could be considered a representative of the American intelligentsia who had read the classics, the contemporary theories about race, and the essays on ancient Egyptian civilization, its origin and the role played by black Africa in the development of the civilizations of the Nile Valley. As to the last issue, his opinion was clear-cut and preconceived:

> "Those friends of the African race
> who point to Egypt as a proof of
> what that race has accomplished are
> wholly mistaken. The only negro
> features represented in Egyptian
> sculpture were those of slaves and
> captives taken in the Ethiopian
> wars of the Pharaohs.[25]

He went on to say that there was no evidence in the Nile Valley that the Negro race had achieved any higher civilization than that exhibited in the Congo and among the Ashantee.

Concerning the tribes that inhabited Northern Sudan, Taylor believed that they migrated from Arabia, and that "there had been very little admixture with the races beyond Sennar, who are looked upon as little better than wild beasts."[26]

His remarks reflect a significant and subtle shift in the debate between the supporters and opponents of slavery in the United States. The question was no longer the legality or illegality of slavery, but the eligibility of the Negro race, and its contribution, or lack or contribution, to the achievements of mankind. Taylor's position was definitely similar to those who, prior to and at the time of the publication of his book, stigmatized the Negro race as culturally and intellectually deprived. His argument also reveals the impact of the discovery of the Nile Valley civilizations on the intellectuals of the period.

Another American who traveled to the northern borders of the Sudan in the same year of Taylor's visit was Dr. Jerome Smith, editor of the Boston Medical and Surgical Journal. If Taylor represented the American intellectual in the social sciences, Smith represented him in the natural sciences. His book, Pilgrimage to Egypt (1852), records his observations and commentaries.

Dr. Smith described the town of Assuan, on the border between Egypt and Sudan, as being the first slave market for slaves from Sudan and Central Africa. He added that slaves were registered, and a custom tax was collected on each individual. According to Smith, the government income from such taxes was considerable.[27]

Smith was interested in the castration of young slave boys to meet the increased demand in the Muslim world for eunuchs. He wrote that nearly all the eunuchs brought to market were from the interior of Africa, and that the Coptic priests in Abyssinia had been accused of performing the operations. He argued that because twenty percent of the operations resulted in death, the price of a eunuch was so high that only the wealthy could afford to purchase one. As to the two French surgeons performing the operations at the time in the Dongola region of the Sudan, he wrote that "their murderous cruelty, which consigns hundreds to the grave in the very spring-tide of life, should be brought to an end, if it is possible for Christian or political influences to reach them."[28]

POST-CIVIL WAR TRAVELERS TO EGYPT AND SUDAN

Mark Twain visited Egypt in 1867. By this time
the slave trade was a clandestine underground business
in both Cairo and Constantinople, where the writer
stopped for a short while on his way to Egypt. He
remarked that the slave trade markets "no more existed."
But in his satirical way, he invented a commercial
report, similar to those published in American newspapers for other commodities:

> ---- Slave-girl Market Reports ----
> Best brands Circassians, crops 1850,
> £250; 1854, £300. Best brands,
> Georgian, none in the market; second
> quality, 1851, £180. Nineteen fair
> to middling Wallachian girls offered
> at £150, but no takers; sixteen
> prime, all sold in small lots to
> close out - terms private.
>
> ...His Majesty the Sultan has already
> sent in large order for his new
> harem, which will be finished within
> a fortnight, and this has naturally
> strengthened the market and given
> Circassian stock a strong upward
> tendency. Taking advantage of the
> inflated market, many of our shrewdest
> operators are selling short. There
> are hints of a "corner" on Wallachians.
>
> There is nothing new in Nubians.
> Slow sale.
>
> Eunuchs - non offering; however,
> large cargoes are expected from Egypt
> today.[29]

More seriously, the author reported that Circassian
and Georgian girls were sold in Constantinople by their
starving parents "simply to save themselves and the
girls from dying of want. It is sad to think of so
distressing a thing as this, and I for one am sincerely
glad the prices are up again."[30]

Mark Twain, like most of the American travelers
before him, displayed no outrage or even concern about
the sale of white women as slaves at a time when white
supremacy was taken for granted in the United States.

In 1869, the American journalist and correspondent to the New York Herald, and secretary of the American Geographical Society, Alvan S. Southworth, visited the Sudan and stayed in Khartoum for several months in order to explore the subject of the slave trade in the Nile Valley. His subsequent book contained the most extensive information written by an American writer about the subject of the slave trade and slavery in the Sudan.

In addition to scattered information on the subject throughout his account, Southworth wrote an entire chapter on the slave trade, including valuable statistics. According to him, the slave trade was the backbone of the Sudanese economy at the time. Loans were obtained at Khartoum at the "exhorbitant interest rate of five to twelve percent montly or 60 to 144 per annum. All the Egyptian salaried clerks who get above 40 Egyptian pounds a month are enabled to lend in this manner, and in a year's time, they find they have a snug profit."[31]

Southworth reported that each dealer had his own territory in Southern Sudan, and resented any attempt of another trader to trespass thereon. He told of the Egyptian merchant, Agad, the most notorious of all slave traders, who knew of, and whose men frequently visited, the Victoria Nyanza region long before the expedition of Speke and other celebrated European explorers.

Southworth estimated the number of slaves "from the country lying between the Red Sea to the Great Desert" at 25,000 annually, and distributed as follows: From Abyssinia, carried to Jaffa or Gallabat, 10,000; issuing by other routes of Abyssinia, 5,000; by the Blue Nile, 3,000; by the White Nile, 7,000. He added that in transporting the 25,000 slaves to market, 15,000 died before reacing their destination, "and often the mortality reaches the terrible figure of 50,000. It is a fair estimate to say that 50,000 children are stolen from their parents every year by persons who have the names and reputation of being civilized and educated."[32] Of those 25,000 slaves, Southworth reported that 15,000 were males, 10,000 females; and that upon reaching Egypt, they met with various fates, as shown in the following table:

```
Finally are made soldiers -----------   6,000
Finally become concubines
(nearly all women) ------------------   2,000
After leaving state of concubinage
are married -------------------------   9,000
Become cooks and servants -----------   5,000
Die from the climate ---------------- 10,000
Are made eunuchs --------------------     500
Finally become educated -------------   1,000
Obtain a competency -----------------      10
Obtain their papers of freedom ------   3,000
Become Christians -------------------    none
Are contented with their final lot,
because of ignorant of a better
existence --------------------------- 20,000
```

/33

As for their prices, Southworth presented the
following list in "Austrian" dollars, which he estimated
to be about the value of a Mexican dollar:

```
For raw negro boys, from the White
Nile, eight years of age --------------   40
For raw negro girls from the White
Nile, eight years of age --------------   60
For men taught to work, twenty five
years of age -------------------------  150
For women, negroes, twenty-five years
of age -------------------------------  100
For Abyssinian girl, ten years old -----  60
For Abyssinian girl, twelve years
old, ordinary looking ----------------  100
For Abyssinian girl, fourteen years
old, fine looking --------------------  150
For Abyssinian girl, fourteen years
old, beautiful -----------------------  200
For Abyssinian girl, fourteen years
old, beautiful (White) ---------------  300
Women beyond seventeen are not in
demand but when sold, if concubines,
bring --------------------------------  100
Old slaves, seldom sold, it being a
point of honor not to send an aged
survivor adrift ----------------------   50
For eunuch, ordinary, coal black ------  250
For eunuch of the first class ---------  300
```

/34

At one point during his stay, Southworth actually purchased an Abyssinian girl, called Brilla, and manumitted her. He obtained her freedom papers and certified them at the American Consular Agency in Khartoum.[35]

Southworth expressed his belief that the Khedive Ismail's government was serious in its efforts to suppress the slave trade, not only to earn the good will of Western powers, but because the Khedive believed "its abolition will be the swiftest mode of reviving the material prospects of his Central African domains."[36]

On his return trip, the author had a lengthy interview with the Khedive, who discussed with him the expedition of Samuel Baker to Equatoria Province and Central Africa. The Khedive was displeased, according to Southworth, because Baker's zeal in suppressing the slave trade led to the disruption of legitimate trade. Southworth recorded the conversation between himself and the Khedive. The following segment is interesting because it reveals the Khedive's attitude toward slavery and the Africans:

> "When Samuel Baker," he continued
> with animation, "went there with his
> large expedition, he found the slave
> trade nearly dead. The suppression
> of that traffic injured our interests
> very much, yet we hoped to save a
> remnant of the commerce with the
> natives. Now all is dead. Peace
> instead of war, cultivation instead
> of conquest, amity instead of
> violence, must be my policy toward
> the peoples of Central Africa. I
> wish to civilize and develop these
> lands, but I cannot do it if the
> blacks are aroused to a bitter op-
> position. The nature of a negro is
> simple, but leave him alone. I regret
> what Sir Samuel Baker has done,
> because it implants in their rude,
> untaught minds that Egypt is their
> enemy. Baker's position is doubtless
> critical."[37]

Charles Dudley Warner journeyed to Egypt in 1874, traveling to the Egyptian-Sudanese borders. He reported that the slave trade still continued between the two countries, but on a smaller scale, because of the Khedive's efforts. He related the story of the Abyssinian boy who accompanied their group. The boy said he had come to Cairo through Mecca in Arabia, Warner explaining that Mecca was another route that the slave traders used.[38]

The sight of the ancient monuments and the achievements of the ancient civilizations of the Nile Valley prompted Warner to speculate on the origin of the ancient Egyptians and the contribution of the Africans. His comments throw some light on the contemporary state of anthropological studies and the deep-rooted animosity and hatred of the Negro race in the United States. He called the land beyond Ethiopia "the vast, black cloud of Negroland," and its inhabitants, "these negroes, with the crisp, wooly hair," who "did not descend from anybody, according to the last reports; neither from Shem, Ham, or Japhet."[39] He further described the population as a motley mixture of different races with no two individuals carrying the same feature. As to Ahmad, a Nubian servant, "the negro blood comes out in him in his voice and laugh and a certain rolling antic movement of his body."[40]

The former American agent and consul-general in Egypt, 1853-61, Edwin de Leon, a South Carolinian, who had resigned his post at the outbreak of the Civil War to become the Confederacy's diplomatic representative in Europe, visited Egypt in 1877. In the same year, his book entitled, The Khedive's Egypt: The Old House of Bondage Under New Masters, was published. In it, de Leon claimed that the Khedive Ismail was genuine in his attempt to suppress the slave trade, the evidence being the absolute authority he delegated to Gordon Pasha as Governor-General of the Sudan. He added, however, that he did not know which of the two tasks Gordon had set for himself was the more difficult to accomplish, being that the Central or Equatorial Africans were "terribly barbarous and savage, and as faithless and ferocious, with a wild sense of independence, and hatred of all the restraints of civilization;" and that slavery and the slave trade have "long been cherished institutions of the country, the very foundation of their social system." He concluded that Gordon, even without entirely accomplishing

41

his task, might reduce the existing chaos and pave the way for "at least the partial civilization of a people, at present given over to barbarism."[41]

De Leon included an entire chapter concerning the Sudan, in which he defended the Khedive's expansionist policies in Central Africa. He stated that Ismail had inherited the Sudan from his grandfather, Mohammed Ali, who conquered it to introduce legitimate trade and civilization to the Negroes of Central Africa; but that unfortunately, they had become the victims of slavers who turned Khartoum into an important slave market, with the complicity and blessing of the government officials. He added that the Sudan was from the start a mere decoration, void of any economic value, and it was doubtful that Egypt would ever reap any profit in return for whatever efforts and expenses she incurred on herself during the process of conquering and ruling it.

He presented seven suggestions to save the deteriorating situation in Egypt. The sixth dealt with uplifting the position of the fellah (peasant). The seventh dealt with the slave trade and slavery in Egypt, in which he recommended its abolition in light of the fact that "only domestic slavery exists there, and is half abolished already." With its abolition, he believed, "many of the social evils existing there would be ameliorated;" but that "in the present condition of the country, the initiatory steps in such reforms would have to be taken under foreign tutelage. There is already a small educated class of natives, and so quick-witted a race as the Egyptian, can soon be taught sufficient to take at least a part in self-government."[42]

The link of the slaves' position in Egypt with that of the Egyptian fellaheen, or serfs, and women appear in several of the American accounts of the Egyptian society in the nineteenth century. Although the social stigma is limited to the black slaves, economically, they were not worse off than the fellaheen, and less exploited than Egyptian women.

In March of 1887, Frederick Douglass, the ex-slave abolitionist, orator, and diplomat, visited Egypt with his wife to see the monuments of its ancient civilizations, which, he remarked gloatingly, were constructed when Europe was "inhabited by barbarians." Confessing that his motive for visiting Egypt was less than sentimental, Douglass said that he had "an ethnological purpose in the pursuit of which I hoped to turn my visit to some account in combating American prejudice against the darker colored races of mankind, and at the same time to raise colored people somewhat in their own estimation and thus stimulate them to higher endeavors." He continued by saying that he had a theory for which "I wanted the support of facts in the range of my knowledge."[43]

We have already discussed Bayard Taylor's and Charles Dudley Warner's works, and pointed out how they manipulated the achievements of the civilizations of the Nile Valley to strip the Negro race of any contribution or input. Both writers had divided the population of the Nile Valley into Negroes, and others; and that the only role played by the Negroes, according to them, was that of slaves. Douglass, in turn, divided the world into two races: the white and darker races, and assigned the achievements of the Nile Valley civilization to the latter, in which the Negro was the basic element.

He discovered a striking similarity between Egyptian workers and black workers in the United States, remarking to himself, "You fellows are at least in your disposition, half brothers to Negroes." As for the Egyptians in general, he stated, "In color, those Arabs are something between two riding saddles, the one old and the other new. They are a little lighter than the one, and a little darker than the other."[44]

Douglass spoke of Islam with respect, something non-existent in the writings of his white compatriots. Apparently he and his wife felt deep emotional ties with the Egyptians; and in 1898, his wife sent an autographed copy of his memoirs to the Khedive through the State Department, which instructed its Agent and Consul-General in Cairo to see it that the monarch received the book.

Chapter III

THE MOLDING OF PUBLIC OPINION

By 1863 the attack on the slave trade in the Ottoman Empire, as well as that on slavery in America, had come to a successful conclusion. In 1841, the slave trade had been officially abolished in all Ottoman territory by the Convention signed by the British Government and Sultan Abdul Majid. In 1857, a _firman_ was issued which declared the "final abolition of the negro slave trade with a view to the extinction of slavery itself throughout the Sultan's dominions."[1] In 1863 slavery was abolished in the United States. The energies of the British Anti-Slavery Society were now free on two major fronts and were directed to East and Northeast Africa and the Sudan, where the slave trade was still energetically pursued. European missionaries and explorers had exposed the situation in the Southern Sudan to the outside world and supplied the British Anti-Slavery Society and its supporters with the needed ammunition to intensify their pressure on the British and Egyptian governments to suppress the slave trade in the Nile Valley.

In contrast, the American anti-slavery societies were not able to continue their struggle to suppress the last pockets of slavery outside the United States, or to perceive a role for their government or for American religious and social organizations in the suppression of the slave trade in the Nile Valley. Immediately after the Civil War, the American anti-slavery movement had begun to disintegrate, soon to vanish from the political and social scene in the United States. The long, bitter and divisive civil strife had consumed its energies and momentum, and emptied it of its moral content. The trauma of the Civil War, and the hard feelings that resulted from it--legacies that only the soul of a slave society can experience--must have been behind the American reluctance to get involved in a situation which would have necessarily opened the tender wounds of the recent past. The American society at the time was rolling on the bumpy and uncertain road of Reconstruction.

Even long before the Civil War, however, the American government had been reluctant to reach an agreement with Great Britain to suppress the slave trade.

Finally in 1842, the Webster-Ashburton Treaty was signed. The creation of a combined African Squadron to inspect and stop the traffic was one of the provisions of the treaty.

Alan R. Booth who studied the role played by the American concluded that the squadron was not a success as an instrument of suppression of the slave trade, having captured in eighteen years only twenty-four ships and liberating a total of 4,945 slaves. During the same years, the British West African Squadron captured 595 ships, liberating 45,612 Africans. Booth attributes the lack of success to the fact that most of the United States Navy Secretaries during the period were not personally interested in stopping the slave trade. Six of the nine Secretaries who held office during the period came from the South. Only one Northern Secretary, George Bancroft, actively supported abolition. The remaining two were Southern sympathizers.[2]

Some American newspapers covered the developments in the Nile Valley surprisingly consistently, although their coverage depended solely on British sources, and their commentaries were colored by the influence of the British anti-slavery rhetoric and arguments.

The outbreak of the Mahdia in 1881 increased the interest of the American press in the question of slavery and the slave trade in the Nile Valley. In the white press, the Mahdi was generally portrayed as a notorious slave trader, and his revolt as one aimed against the suppression of the slave trade. Later, after the fall of Khartoum at the hands of the Mahdi, he and his followers were hailed as nationalists and champions of the Arab race." The Black press was confused and ambivalent. On one hand, it hailed the Mahdi as a black hero; while on the other hand, it was repelled by his image as a slave trader.

THE WHITE PRESS

In June of 1867 a delegation of anti-slavery societies in England and France had an interview with the Khedive Ismail during his visit to Paris. The British Anti-Slavery Reporter of July 15, 1867 published a report of the interview. Two months later, the New York Times published a similar report.[3]

46

According to the paper, the Khedive attacked the
European merchants who were engaged in the slave trade
while raising their national flags on their boats.
Because of the Capitulation Regime that protected
Europeans from prosecution within local jurisdictions
throughout the Ottoman Empire, the Khedive and his
government were powerless in this situation. The
Khedive urged the European governments to give him the
right to search and detain these boats and their owners
and crew; in other words to help him obtain his
independence from the Ottoman Empire. But the European
governments and especially England were committed to
the survival of the Ottoman Empire, the sick man of
Europe. The New York Times commented that the members
of the delegation, no doubt, differed with Khedive's
argument that the slave trade was the source of slavery
in his domains, and that its suppression meant the end
of slavery.

Very little attention was given by the New York
Times to the slave trade during the following eight
years. These were the years that witnessed the most
dramatic increase in the slave trade and in the pressure
from the British Anti-Slavery Society. In 1869 the
Khedive Ismail had appointed Samuel Baker to establish
an effective administration in Southern Sudan, expand
the Khedive's dominions further south to the Lakes
region, and suppress the slave trade. The slavers
conceived this step, correctly, as a threat to their
political and economic domination of the region. It is
unfortunate that this important period received scant
coverage in the New York Times.

In August of 1874, the paper published an editorial
under the title, "Egypt, the Cotton Crop and the Slave
Trade," based on an article that appeared in the London
Times. The New York Times expressed an interest in
the "letters which have lately appeared in the Times
concerning the slave trade on Egyptian territory."[4]

A month later the paper published another article
based on despatches that appeared in the London Times
announcing the capture by Egyptian authorities in
southern Kordofan of a large slave caravan. It gave
a detailed description of slave routes across the
desert in Sudan.[5]

In February of 1875, the New York Times published
a lengthy editorial about the occupation of Darfur,

its annexation to the Egyptian domains, and the
historical significance of such action. The article
characterized Africa in general as "a perpetual monu-
ment of human barbarism, and Equatorial Africa in
particular as "the running sore of the world."[6]
The same editorial mentioned the British efforts in
the west and on the southern coasts of Africa, conceding
that as far as Equatorial Africa was concerned, "The
only power that could by any possibility benefit this
portion of Africa is Egypt."[7] Nevertheless, the
writer saw in the suppression of the slave trade and
the introduction of legitimate trade, a commercial
benefit to the United States: "The simple tools and
manufactures of England and America would pour into
these unknown regions, to be exchanged for ivory and
other tropical products."[8]

In November of 1877, the New York Times referred
to the despatch of Elbert E. Farman, the American
Agent and Consul-General in Egypt, to the United States
State Department, dated August, 1877, concerning the
Convention between Egypt and Great Britain for the
Suppression of the Slave Trade, signed at Alexandria
in August of 1877.[9] The story was published under
the headline: "The Slave Traffic in Egypt--No Sale
for Africans and Abyssinians, But Trade in Circassians
and Georgians Still Tolerated." The title reflects
the caustic criticism by Farman of the Convention,
namely that although the Convention referred specifically to Negro and Abyssinian slaves, it mentioned
nothing about the Circassian and Georgia (white)
female slaves. The inference of the Consul-General
and the newspaper was correct. The paper remarked:

> Whenever the word slaves occurs
> it is immediately qualified by the
> words "Africans or Abyssinians"
> which qualification it would seem,
> was intended to exclude from the
> terms of that instrument the
> Circassian and Georgian female
> slaves, who are purchased in Con-
> stantinople by the middle and
> upper classes in Egypt and held in
> harems under the designation of
> servants and wives. These "servants"
> with whom the masters live in a
> state of concubinage, and who are
> only limited in number by the desire

48

and wealth of the purchasers, are
really slaves, but it is clear from
the wording of the Convention that
while the severest measures will be
adopted for the suppression of the
African and Abyssinian slavery, the
oriental system which condemns the
beautiful white women of Georgia
and Circassia to lives of slavery
and concubinage will not be interfered
with in any manner whatever.[10]

Although the comment is an echo of Farman's
despatch, its publication in an American newspaper, and
at an extremely critical time in the history of the
confrontation between the southern whites and blacks
on one hand, and between the supporters and detractors
of blacks on the other hand, was tantamount to adding
fuel to an already vigorous fire. Early in that year,
the Republican and Democratic parties had reached an
agreement to withdraw Federal troops from the South,
thus bringing the Reconstruction period to an end,
and giving the Southern extremists a free hand in
taking away the rights which the blacks had obtained
since the end of the Civil War. To publish the story
in such an atmosphere and time, and under that title,
was the death knell to any possibility that the
United States government would have any part, directly
or indirectly, in suppressing slavery and the slave
trade in "Negroes and Abyssinians in the Nile Valley,"
while white women were still in bondage.

Six weeks later, the newspaper published another
article by an "Occasional Correspondent" concerning
the slave trade in Egypt. The writer predicted that
the Convention "valuable as it is, will prove a
failure," as long as the demand for slaves from
Constantinople continued. The Correspondent then
turned to Great Britain, vessels from which country
it said, carried slaves surreptitiously from Tunis
to Constantinople and elsewhere, allegedly without
seizure in spite of the violation of British law. He
reported:

Last year more than 20,000 slaves
were carried away from one little
port in the dominion of the Sultan
of Zanzibar....Baker was received
into (or, as they now had it round
the palace, imposed upon) his

49

Highness' service in 1869 and after
four years of fighting with the
natives in Central Africa succeeded,
is asked, In What? Not in destroying
the slave trade which he made the
primary object of his expedition,
nor in opening up with the tribes
of the region peaceful communication
and trade, which the Khedive so much
desired; but he did succeed, at least
his measures resulted, in driving
the game into British nets at and
near Zanzibar.[11]

The article continued by saying that the slave
trade and ivory trade were "hand and glove." In the
beginning of his despatch, the "Occasional Correspondent"
had referred to his recent article in the New York Times,
the only one about Egypt and the slave trade being the
one by Farman, published on November 11, 1877 criticizing the Convention. It is difficult to resist the
temptation to conclude that the writer of both articles
was Farman, whose despatches and published works showed
that he was a devout Anglophobe, and an admirer of the
Khedive Ismail. If this conclusion is correct, the
Farman was working on two levels--official and public--
to undermine any participation of the United States in
any effort to suppress the slave trade in the Nile
Valley at the time.[12]

In a lengthy editorial in August of 1881, the New
York Times discussed the slave trade in the Nile Valley,
lamenting the absense of any reliable statistics due to
the reluctance of slavers to disclose the number of
their slaves in order to protect their interests, and
because statistics was unknown to the Arabs. The
editorial added that after the departure of Gordon, the
slave trade began to flourish anew. According to it,
it was believed that between sixty and seventy thousand
slaves were carried through the Egyptian and Ottoman
ports annually; and that this was a shameful situation,
especially because it was possible to eradicate that
ungodly traffic. The paper reported that if Gordon and
Gessy had got the support they needed, they could have
suppressed the slave trade.[13] The news that the British
government was ready to take the necessary steps to end
the slave trade by posting consuls in the various ports
on the Red Sea was welcomed by the paper. If suitable
men were chosen, it said, they would put enough pressure
on the procrastinating oriental officials.[14]

50

Another item of news that the New York Times
hailed in the same editorial was the Khedive's consent
to call on the highest Islamic religious leaders in
the land to issue a decree to outlaw the slave trade
in Egypt and its dominions. The Khedive's action
was not prompted, according to the paper, by his
interest in rendering a service to humanity, but in
protecting his own interests; and that the influence
and power of the slave traders had reached a point
that constituted a threat to his own authority. The
article concluded by saying that Gordon was not there
anymore, otherwise those two steps would have helped
him to suppress the traffic for good.[15]

The first military confrontation between the Mahdi
and his followers and the Turco-Egyptian government
took place in August of 1881. The first mention of it
in the New York Times was in October of 1882. The
article was based on the accounts of George Schweinfurth
(1838-1925), the German naturalist and traveler, who
visited the Sudan several times and wrote about the
slave trade. The article reported that the Mahdi had
killed eight hundred Egyptian soldiers; and described
him as the notorious slave trader who continued to
resist the government under Gordon in the regions of
Nubia and Sudan for three years.[16]

The paper's reliance on Schweinfurth, who was one
of the main contributors to the British anti-slavery
publications about slavery in the Nile Valley,
influenced its attitude toward the Mahdia; namely
that the Mahdi and his followers were discontented
slavers who were frustrated by the suppression of the
slave trade.

An editorial of January 1884 attacked the British
policy of evacuation of the Sudan. It argued that:

>It was generally understood that the
>Mahdi, prior to his assumption of the
>prophetic title, was a large slave-
>dealer, and that he was prompted to
>rebel against the Khedive in the
>effort made by the Egyptian Government
>to suppress the slave trade in Soudan.
>The English people and government
>brought greater pressure to bear
>upon the Khedive Ismail to break up
>this traffic in human beings than any

European nation and they were
therefore to a certain extent
responsible for the present state
of affairs in the Soudan. Yet
at the same time they were willing
to hold the fertile country they
so easily conquered, while they
shrink from the task of restoring
order in a district where rebel
leaders flew to arms in order to
revive the slave trade.[17]

One month later, the paper published another
editorial concerning the arrival of Gordon to Khartoum
and his proclamation recognizing the Mahdi as Sultan
of Kordofan, cancelling half of the taxes and lifting
all restrictions on the slave trade. The paper went
on to say that if Gordon had really granted freedom
for the slave trade, with the consent of the British
government, he need not have gone to Khartoum at all.
It also demanded that the British Government make
her position clear concerning Gordon's proclamation.
In disbelief, the editorial concluded by saying that
either the despatch was false or Gordon had been acting
on his own account.[18]

Another editorial on the same subject followed,
stating that Gordon "may have passed the narrow line
which, in come cases, divides religious exaltation
from lunacy." As to Gordon's act of releasing the
prisoners in Khartoum and the burning of the jail, the
editorial asked how a sane man could imagine that a
town like Khartoum, inhabited "by the worst ruffians
that the slave trade has produced, be kept in order
without a jail?" The editorial rejected the explanation that Gordon's legalization of the slave trade
was a mere measure of expedience.[19]

Referring to the defeat of Osman Digna in early
1884, an editorial sarcastically and scornfully said
that the "infatuated creatures" who have enlisted
under the banner of the "false prophet" believed that
they were invulnerable and that they bore charmed lives
while in the service of the Mahdi. It assessed the
number of those killed and wounded to be six thousand.[20]

The attacks on the British government were
becoming a permanent feature. The paper charged that
the lack of a policy had led to the entrapment of

Gordon in Khartoum. It argued prophetically that the Mahdi would never lift the seige of the city before getting "possession of the head of the only man who ventured to pose as his rival." Gladstone was held responsible by the editor for the pending loss of the Sudan and the death of Gordon.[21]

Unaware of the fall of Khartoum, on January 25, 1885, the New York Times published an editorial praising the efforts of the British government to save Gordon. It launched its most vicious attack on the Mahdi and his followers, saying:

> Stewart was the representative of civilization in a struggle with Barbarism. The forces opposed to him are not, like the Afghans or the Zulus or the Boers, men merely defending their native country against an invasion of conquest. They are a gang of the meanest of all thieves--slave thieves, namely, they have converted their habitat, by nature a desert, into a slum, and abject vices are in no degree redeemed by their fanaticism. So far as they are concerned there is no room for sympathy.[22]

After the fall of Khartoum and the assassination of Gordon, the paper's attitude toward the Mahdia began to change. The Mahdi and his followers were from then on considered as nationalists, and the British as arrogant intruders. The British became the target of the editor's wrath: "The domineering temper which inspires these monstrous claims is the explanation why the English are the best-hated people on the face of the earth." The British claims and atrocities in Ireland, India, and South Africa were also cited.[23]

One week later, the Mahdi was described in an editorial entitled, "Arab Esau and Turkish Jacob," as the champion of the Arab race against the hated Turks who had usurped the "birth-right of the Arab Esau" to the Islamic Empire.[24]

The victory of the Mahdi was welcomed by the Irish community in the United States, and stories about sending an Irish brigade to the Sudan to join the Mahdi under General Fitzhugh were circulating in Chicago. The <u>New York Times</u> dismissed the stories as rumors. Nevertheless, it admitted that:

> There were reckless and restless
> men in the South and West who might
> join such an expedition, but it is
> certain that no man who has anything
> to lose will be found among them.

The editorial went on to enumerate the insurmountable difficulties of reaching the Sudan. It argued that since the Egyptian government would not allow an Irish brigade into the Sudan, the only other alternative would be to capture either Alexandria or Suakin by force.[25]

With the same vigor, the paper dismissed rumors circulating in the British press about the rise of a rival Mahdi, labeling them as mere delusion. It advised the British to take the Mahdi seriously.

> Should the brave Osman Digna take
> Suakin there is little to prevent
> a prophetical progress of the
> Mahdi to Mecca, and once Safely in
> Mecca, it is only possible that
> the whole Moslem world, Northern
> India and Ceylon included, will
> rise in his name....

> The Mahdi of the Sudan is not dead.
> He is a lion by no means fangless;
> he is now quiet, but it is safe to
> be sure that he is not asleep.[26]

In another editorial, the Sudan was described as potentially a collection of heterogeneous races, who were easily defeated and controlled by the Egyptians. The Mahdi was given credit for uniting them into "one oppressing force." His untimely death was seen as a prelude to the disintegration of the Sudan. Britain, France, Turkey, Italy, and Abyssinia were alluded to as "watching the opportunities of this state of anarchy." According to the editorial, the failure of any of these powers, individually or collectively, to take advantage of the situation on one hand, and the subsiding of the furor in England caused by the death of Gordon and the fall of Khartoum on

the other hand, gradually helped to push the Sudan
away from the center of the stage.[27] Little was said
about it in the New York Times until 1898, when it
emerged again as a bone of contention among rival
European powers.

Between the fall of Khartoum at the hands of the
Mahdists in January of 1885, and the fall of Omdurman
at the hands of the Anglo-Egyptian troops in September
of 1898, the American attitude toward the question
of colonialism had changed considerably. The United
States had become a colonial power, using more or less
the same methods and justifications used by other
colonial powers. The defeat of the Khalifa and the
number of casualties were reported from a social
Darwinist point of view. After giving the figures
of 10,000 killed and 16,000 wounded in the Mahdidst
armies, and 47 killed and 342 wounded in the Anglo-
Egyptian troops, the New York Times in an editorial
added contemptuously that

> The Sudanese can hardly be said
> to have had any training or leadership
> at all, and their weapons, though
> a little more modern than stone
> axes, were hopelessly antiquated
> in comparison with the newest of
> magazine rifles and machine guns.
> The blind ferocity of the Mahdists
> availed them nothing, for they could
> not come within striking distance
> of their hated foes.

As for the large number of casualties among the
Mahdists and whether Anglo-Egyptian commanders had been
vindictive, the editorial was both defensive and
apologetic. According to it, battles in which the
slaughter was all on one side had been not infrequent
"when civilization was in conflict with barbarism."[28]

As to the racial identity of the Mahdi and his
followers, the New York Times frequently referred to
them as Arabs, while calling those enslaved "Negroes."
The Mahdi and his followers were referred to as being
of the same race as the Egyptians.[29] The same editorial
commented on the rise of another Mahdi, describing
him as being black as his rival.[30] As to his claim
of being the descendant of Prophet Mohammed, the paper
said: "He is not of pure Arab stock, nor can he boast
of the ancient ecclesiastical family of Mohammed."[31]

After the defeat of the Khalifa, the paper referred to the Mahdists as the "big black bounding beggars."[32] When Great Britain decided to abandon the Sudan in 1884, the <u>New York Times</u> wrote:

> England has never had any real business in the Sudan. To combine the suppression of the slave trade with the extension of British markets is a program which appeals to both the finest and the coarsest feelings of the English middle class....It seems to be going altogether too far...to take possession of an unwholesome desert for the purpose of enabling her to prevent Arabs from selling negroes to Egyptians. This sudden and extreme sensibility about the right of the weak, when the strong happen to be Arab slave-traders, is at once comic and pathetic, considering the recent attitude of Britain in the Transvaal and Afghanistan. Solicitude for the welfare of a people for whose condition Britain is not responsible is accompanied with profound indifference to the welfare of people for whose condition Britain is responsible.
>
> The abandonment of Sudan, especially since it has become evident that there is no money in it, is therefore the dictate of common sense. But Britain cannot abandon Gordon without national dishonor.[33]

THE BLACK PRESS

The attention of the West was drawn to the Nile Valley in the nineteenth century by two developments. The first was the discovery of the greatness of the ancient Nile Valley civilizations. The second was the increase of the slave trade in the second half of the century, after the opening of the Upper Nile provinces. These two developments came at a time when the controversy over the issue of slavery and the contribution of the African to civilization was at its height

56

in the United States. Both sides of the controversy made use of the two developments to defend their points of view. The fact that the Nile Valley was inhabited by a mixture of races helped to widen and obscure the controversy.

For the black American, the controversy was more than just an intellectual exercise. While he was proud of the great achievements of the civilization, he was confused and embarassed by the slave trade. While he could easily relate to the ancient inhabitants of the Nile Valley and identify with them, he was alienated by the actions of their descendants. The fact that the slave traders were referred to as "Arab" and "Muslims," and the slaves were identified as "Negroes" and "non-Muslims" left him in a dilemma.

The rise of the Mahdi and the increasing coverage of his revolution by the Western press, especially after the involvement of Gordon, could not be ignored by the black press. Since the main source of infor- mation was the biased British press, the black American's confusion over the terminology was further aggravated. The Mahdi was referred to variously as an "Arab," "African," "Muslim," and the leader of "slave traders." The black American press' attitude toward him was a mixture of trust, hate, and admiration.

At first the label "false prophet" was applied to the Mahdi automatically. After the total annihil- ation of Hicks Pasha's expedition in November of 1883, the attitude of the black press toward the Mahdi began to change. Early in 1884, the New York Age carried an editorial which said:

> This bold African chief leads a
> movement to throw off the odious
> yoke of Egyptian misrule. He has
> arrayed under his banner all the
> malcontent tribes of the Nile
> country. It is to be regretted
> that the English government should
> deem it necessary to interfere
> with local concerns of Egypt and
> her dissatisfied colonies....We
> sincerely hope that the False
> Prophet will carry slaughter and
> havoc into the British forces
> bent against him, for England has

no more right to oppose him than
has our government.[34]

When Gordon declared in Berber in February of 1884
that the Anglo-Egyptian Convention of 1877, concerning
the liberation of the Sudan, would not be implemented,
the reaction of the New York Age was instant. It said:

> This startling proclamation from
> a nation we have believed to be the
> champion of freedom has much interest
> for the intelligent colored people
> all over the world.[35]

In the following week, the paper published the
first of two articles by Archibald Johnson, a black
scholar studying in London, entitled, "Slavery in
Egypt." After discussing slavery in Egypt and North
Africa, and the failure of Christianity to do anything
about it, he called upon the black Americans and the
Pope to move and eliminate slavery. Addressing the
black Americans, he said:

> The subject needs no apology to
> colored Americans, for they cannot
> avoid giving their sympathy to
> the unfortunate portion of our
> race that is still held in the
> thrall and meshes of slavery....
>
> Slavery must be wholly blotted out
> of the world woes: no people has
> greater right to emblazen that
> fact before the world than the
> colored people of America.[36]

Johnson failed to point out what the black people of
America could do to stop slavery in the Nile Valley,
nor did he refer to the Mahdi and what he thought of
him.

After the fall of Khartoum and the emergence of
the Mahdist state, the black press began to take a
closer look at the Mahdi. The New York Freeman argued
that the Mahdi was improperly referred to as a
Sudanese, when he was "a Nubian by birth, by education
and social ties." Bilad es Sudan, the Land of the
Blacks, or Negritis, was identified by the paper as
that tract of Central Africa extending for 2,500,000
square miles in which the Mahdi planned to spread Islam.

58

Nubia was occupied by Egypt, according to the paper, in order to reach Central Africa for slaves. The number of African slaves captured every year was given as one million. Only one-fifth of them survived the hardships of the route to the markets of North America, and the Middle East. The middlemen of the slave trade were the Nubians who became so strong that they threatened to swallow the authority of the Khedive, who appealed to Gordon for help. The employment of Gordon exasperated the Nubians, the middlemen on whom Egypt could depend in case of an emergency. They rose under the Mahdi to protect their interests in the slave trade.[37]

The Mahdi was described by the paper as a pious man with a shrewd eye for business. According to the paper:

> In 1878 he had become so wealthy
> that he felt the necessity to
> declare that Allah had ordered him
> to leave his silo and take unto
> himself a large collection of
> wives, whom, as a truly practical
> man, he chose among the most influ-
> ential families of the country,
> especially that of the Bagara, the
> most opulent slave-traders in the
> White Nile....On the other hand,
> his program answered all the
> aspirations of millions of helpless
> and downtrodden Negroes, and served
> at the same time the old grudges
> of the slave-traders--that is, the
> middle and ruling classes of Sudan--
> against the successor of Mohamet Ali.[38]

One week later, the <u>Freeman</u> attacked Britain for interfering in the Sudan, and declared that "our sympathies are with the Sudanese because they fight for independence."[39] When the Mahdi died a few weeks later, the paper eulogized him as a courageous man who protected his homeland from British expansionism.[40] The image of the Mahdi as a liberator of his country prevailed; that of the proselytizer and the slave trader was submerged. The Mahdi was conceived as an African standing up to European intrusion in the continent of their ancestors.

The American press coverage of slavery and the slave trade in the Nile Valley in general, and the Mahdi in particular indicate that while the official interests in the Nile Valley were minimal, the public concerns, both cultural and racial, were many and complex.

The victory of the Mahdi over the Anglo-Egyptian troops transformed the Mahdi in the American press from a "false prophet" to a great nationalist, fighting for the freedom of his people and land. While his patriotism appealed to the white press, his resounding defeat of the British and Egyptian troops appealed to the blacks; yet neither group gave him its full moral support and admiration.

The tendency of the Americans to identify the rest of the world in terms of race and color was frustrated by the marginality of the Sudan, between the Middle East and Africa, and the failure of the Mahdia to forge out an identity other than that of religion.

Chapter IV

AMERICAN MISSIONARIES AND SOLDIERS: ENVOYS OF MODERNIZATION

The American missionaries and army officers who came to the Nile Valley in the nineteenth century played an important role as representatives of the American culture and in the development of the region. The missionaries, initially having hoped to convert Muslims to Christianity, and having discovered that this was unattainable, shifted their focus to converting the Copts to the Western version of Christianity. The resistance of the Copts finally led the missionaries to limit their efforts to education and distribution of the Bible. The missionary contribution in the field of education was great, to the extent that the graduates of their schools constituted a sizable portion of the Egyptian bureaucracy.

The officers brought with them the latest military training and technology. Like the missionaries, they were faced with resistance from both Turco-Egyptian officers and European expatriates; nevertheless, their impact on the reorganization of the Egyptian army, and their contribution in surveying and mapping the new territories acquired in Sudan were essential to the southward expansion of Egypt. In this regard, there was a link between the American missionaries and officers which contributed in no mean way to the Khedive Ismail's efforts of modernization, and aspirations for establishing an independent Nile Valley empire. Whether their efforts helped in abolishing the slave trade in the Nile Valley depends on how we interpret Ismail's priorities in Central Africa: expansionism or abolition of the slave trade.

THE AMERICAN MISSION IN EGYPT

The European immigrants to the New World were faced from the start with the problem of missionary work among the indigenous population and later, among the African slaves. The mere acceptance of the idea of spreading Christianity among both groups implied that the Indian and African were, like the white settlers, in possession of souls to be saved. Such a

61

perception brought about a contradiction in the way these two groups were treated by the settlers. Consequently, the American missionary movement, whether internally, among the indigenous population or African slaves, or externally, among Asians and Africans, was liberal and humanitarian.

After the American Revolution, the movement gained momentum, and began to fight for the abolition of the slave trade and slavery. In this context, the Church found itself divided between a small group that condemned slavery, and an overwhelming majority that condoned it. Quotations from the Bible were used to justify both positions.

When the removal of British domination in America prompted the United States government and merchants to establish independent relations with foreign nations, the American missionaries found a new interest in the outside world. Directly related to this was the development of a new spirit of evangelism, later coupled with the knowledge of the eighteenth century geograph- ical expansion of the British into Asia and Africa, and the British missionary activities among their "pagan" peoples.

In 1810 the American Council for Foreign Missionaries was founded; and the first American mission abroad was established in 1812 in Calcutta, India. Another mission was sent to the Near East in 1818 to work in Jerusalem and Smyrna, attempting to convert the followers of the Eastern Church, Judaism and Islam. Its efforts were not successful; nevertheless the work was considered a challenge. The Nile Valley was not included in this American missionary initiative until the middle of the nineteenth century in spite of the fact that American consular relations were established as early as 1832.

Two missionaries from the American mission in Damascus arrived in Cairo in 1854 to open a branch in that city. Earlier that year Abbas Pasha had been succeeded by Said Pasha as Viceroy of Egypt. Remarked an American missionary concerning this propitious event: "In view of his liberal mind and just reign, there had been no such favorable time for commencing missionary work during the previous 1200 years."[1]

In its first report from Cairo in 1855, the
Mission stated that its activities included Northeast
Africa in an area of three million miles inhabited by
eight million persons. It mentioned that the population lived in different stages of civilization, and
that because of their long oppression, they had lost
individual initiative and self-respect. It stated
that Cairo was chosen because its population was a
quarter of a million, and because of its central
position, which would enable the missionaries to
direct their activities to the different parts of
the region.[2]

The main purpose of the Mission in Egypt was to
gain converts among the Muslims, and to save the Copts
from what it considered to be heresies to the true
Christianity. However, the Mission discovered early
in its activities that it was impossible to work among
the Muslim majority, and limited its scope to the
Coptic minority.

The Coptic Church hierarchy opposed the missionary
influence. The Coptic opposition led to the intervention of the American Agent and Consul-General in
Cairo, William Thayer, on behalf of the Mission; but
he was informed by the Patriarch that the Copts did
not need the effort of the Mission, for they knew
the Bible before the United States was founded.[3]
When the American Mission opened a new center at Asyut,
the spiritual headquarters of the Coptic Church, it
was vigorously resisted; but the American Consul-
General and his European counterparts came to its aid,
as they did whenever Western interests were involved.

When Said Pasha intervened in 1861 to free and
compensate a Christian convert who was attacked by an
angry mob, he received a thankful letter from
Abraham Lincoln. Later in the same year, Said Pasha
gave the Mission in Cairo a building as a gift.[4]
The American government, however, reprimanded its
Consul-General in 1867 for his unwarranted interference
with the Egyptian government in freeing some of the
Mission's converts. His interference, he was told,
was not sanctioned by the Constitution.[5]

The American Mission's activities were geared
to three areas: evangelization, sale of books, and
education; but its success was in reverse order.[6]
The success of the Mission in the field of education

was not to be measured by the number of its students only, but also by the kind of education it was offering in a country that was embarking on a program of modernization. It was reported that in the year 1873, three-quarters of those working in the departments of Post and Telegraph and Railways were graduates of the Mission's schools.[7]

It is evident from all this that the American Mission was enjoying the protection and support of the Egyptian government, and the gratitude of Muslim and Coptic parents whose children were educated in its schools.

Regarding the issue of slavery and the slave trade, it is evident from available sources that the American Mission in Egypt had chosen not to take a position of confrontation against the Egyptian people and government who accepted slavery as a fact of life, and considered pressures to abolish it as an anti-Muslim movement aiming at undermining Egyptian independence and discrediting Islamic institutions. Even the Coptic minority was in agreement with the rest of the Egyptians in this respect. In this sense, the American Mission had chosen a safe and noncontroversial position, so that it could carry on its activities in the fields of evangelization and education.

The official historian of the Mission, the Reverend Andrew Watson, justified its position by maintaining that "Slavery was a legal institution in Egypt when the missionaries came, and the slave-trade, with all its horrors, was in active operation;" and that "The American missionary...at the time could say little against that system of iniquity, since it was still flourishing in the boasted land of liberty, under 'the stars and stripes.'" He characterized slavery in Egypt as perhaps being in "milder form" than slavery in America, but nevertheless condemned it as "the cause of great wrong to the enslaved... and the occasion of great corruption in the homes of the people."[8]

The dilemma of the American Mission in Egypt in relation to the sensitive question of indigenous slavery is indicative of the crisis of a Western Christian institution functioning under the heavy burden of two slave societies which were colliding with one another in the sensitive areas of religion, morality, and conscience. And yet the record of the American Mission in this respect is far superior to that of the Muslim and Coptic religious institutions. Although Muslim Ulma (learned men), and Coptic high priests played an active role in the political turmoils that characterized the political life in Egypt in the nineteenth century, they kept a blissful silence when it came to the horrible practices of the slave trade.[9] Reference has already been made to the Khedive's unsuccessful attempts to induce the Mufti of Islam to issue a decree against slavery and the slave trade.

It would be unfair to the American Mission not to mention its efforts in three areas concerning the slave trade. The first was self-regulatory. Members and supporters of the Mission were not allowed to own slaves. Reverend Watson reported the following story of an Egyptian convert, Tadros Yousif, who was reported to own a slave:

> I took him aside and had a solemn
> talk with him, and tried to show him
> the sin of slavery and the inconsis-
> tence of a Christian holding a human
> being in bondage. He said that he
> had never thought of it before; and
> that he would think about it and pray
> over it that night and let me know
> in the morning what he would do,
> for I had told him we could not go
> on with the ordination until he
> liberated his slave. In the morning
> he announced that he had come to the
> conclusion that it was wrong for a
> Christian to hold a human being in
> bondage, and that he would publicly
> announce the emancipation of his
> slave in the meeting of the congregation
> in the evening, which he did in all
> sincerity.[10]

The second area was in the active role that the Mission played in opening its schools for the young freed slaves to obtain Education and training. One of the despatches of Consul-General E.E. Farman in 1877 mentioned that the Mission had opened a special school for freed slaves.[11] Needless to add, the Mission was fulfilling here its basic function of evangelization: In the absence of any family or master,

those young ex-slaves were automatically converted to
Christianity. The third was the pressure that the
Mission brought to bear on the procrastinating American
consular authorities to help interested slaves in
obtaining their freedom papers. On several occasions,
slaves seeking their freedom papers were brought to
the Consulate-General for action.[12]

Prior to 1898 the American Mission had limited
its work to Egypt proper and did not extend it to the
Sudan until its reconquest in 1898. The Christian
missionary groups after Gordon's death in Khartoum
in 1885 were eager to penetrate the Sudan and avenge
his death through increased proselytization and efforts
to eradicate the slave trade. In June of 1898, the
New York Times published a despatch from Cairo
concerning the impatience of the American Mission to
send its representatives to the Sudan, but that
Lord Kitchener had told them to be patient, and that
they would get permission in due time.[13]

The Reverend Ried F. Shields, the official
historian of the American Mission in the Sudan in the
first third of the twentieth century, wrote that
the slave trade was the only type of commerce that
flourished under the rule of the Mahdia. He added
that the occupation of the ports of Eastern Sudan and
the Red Sea by Italy and Great Britain closed all
outlets for that traffic, and even the Southern
Egyptian borders were closed. As a result the Captured
slaves were sold only in those provinces under the
rule of the Khalifa, and the slave market at Omdurman
became the most important landmark.[14]

For the most part, the American missionary efforts
in the Sudan in general, and toward the suppression
of the slave trade in particular, were relatively
weak until the beginning of the twentieth century,
which is outside the scope of this paper.

AMERICAN OFFICERS IN THE EGYPTIAN ARMY

The Khedive Ismail discovered after six years of
reign that he could not depend on the European powers,
especially Great Britain and France, for the realiza-
tion of his two dreams of full independence from
the Ottoman Empire and geographical expansion into
Central Africa. Both European powers were committed

to the continuation of the status quo as far as the
Ottoman Empire was concerned; and they were not without
their own schemes and ambitions in Africa generally,
and particularly in Northeast and Central Africa.

Determined to realize his two dreams, Ismail
turned to the United States for military ware and
expertise. That country was emerging from a
protracted civil war, and many young, qualified and
able officers had been demobilized. Ismail had four
reasons for using the American officers in training
and modernizing his army. First, the great courage
and perseverance that both Union and Confederate
soldiers had shown during five years (1861-5) of
fighting. Second, the emergence of the United States
as a strong world power following her success in 1867
in forcing Napoleon to withdraw his troops from
Mexico. Third, her lack of political or economic
interests in Egypt. And fourth, the large reservoir
of adverturous and qualified American soldiers.[15]
The concept of using foreign officers to modernize
the Egyptian army was not new to the Egyptian rulers
in the nineteenth century. Mohammed Ali, Ismail's
grandfather, had successfully used French officers
to train his troops in 1819.[16]

Historians differ as to the number of American
officers employed in the Egyptian army. The figures
forty-four, forty-nine, and fifty-five have been
given.[17] They agree, however, that no more than thirty
worked at the same time during the period between
1870 and 1878, when they were fired for financial
reasons, with the exception of General Stone, the
Egyptian army chief-of-staff, who stayed until 1883;
and that they were divided equally between the
Confederate and Union components.

In addition to their wide range of experiences
in the Civil War, a large number of American officers
were graduates of the famous West Point, and other
military and naval academies. A few of them had
already distinguished themselves in their country and
reached high ranks. Some were trained in such technical
skills as engineering, topographical mapping and
surveying, and had acquired many years of experience
on the American frontier. These accomplished skills
proved invaluable to Ismail and his geographical
expansion in Central Africa after 1870. In that
capacity, they explored rivers and lakes; surveyed

whole regions of Northern Sudan to find the shortest
routes for railways; mapped Darfur and Kordofan, and
established friendly relations with the tribal chiefs
along the way.[18]

When the Khedive Ismail met with the first incoming
group of soldiers, he told them that they would find
themselves very soon in the battlefield helping Egypt
to acquire its independence.[19] But the British and
French governments expressed their displeasure to
Nubar Pasha, the Khedive's Chief Minister, at the
employment of the American officers. In 1871 the
Sultan, instigated by Britain and France, sent an
emissary to the Khedive ordering him to dismantle his
coastal defensive installations, which the American
officers had helped to build.[20]

When Samuel Baker, as governor of the Equatorial
Province (1870-1874), and Charles Gordon, first as
governor of that province (1874-1876), and then as
Governor-General of the entire Sudan (1876-1879),
launched the most effective anti-slave trade campaign
in the history of the Nile Valley, the American
officers' efforts constituted an essential part of
that campaign. They worked under both Baker and
Gordon, and did most of the technical work, without
which the campaign would have been of limited success.[21]
Regardless of their positions during the Civil War back
in the United States, or their personal feelings toward
the issue of slavery and the slave trade in the Nile
Valley, they executed their duties fully.

It is unfortunate that these officers left behind
them nothing to indicate their personal feelings toward
the issue of slavery and the slave trade in the Nile
Valley, except such evidence that remained scattered
among the various accounts of their achievements in
the region. One of the American officers who wrote
a book during his sojourn in Egypt was William McE. Dye.
He based his book, <u>Moslem Egypt and Christian Abyssinia</u>
(1880), on reports written by officers Prout, Purdy,
and Colston, who played the important role of surveying
and mapping Darfur and Kordofan. He quoted Colston
as questioning the usefulness of conquering Darfur in
1874:

Under the most favorable circumstances,
the Mohammedan is not a civilizaer;
the felah is not, nor is the negro
sent into that country with arms in
his hand; and when there is added
to these the dregs of Egyptian
society--the worst criminals unexe-
cuted in the land--who are deported
there, the native of necessity
still further sinks in degradation
instead of rising in the scale of
humanity....To maintain many thousands
of these there until such period
arrives with any hope that the
expense of conquest and occupation
can be beaten from the soles of the
For's feet (and preserve, elevate
him at the same time) is worse than
rain--it is imbecility and criminality
exemplified. If one says that
slavery is less, the reply is that
it is unnecessary, and is quite
insane, to kill the patient to cure
the disease. The Khedive should,
like Tiberius, instruct his proconsuls
to shear and not to flay his sheep.[22]

His description of the inhabitants of Jebel Marrah
reflects the anthropological biases of the time, a
few of which were discussed in the first chapter.

These are negroes, black, tall, with
small muscular development, small
heads, big jaws, but higher in the
human scale than the heathen negroes
further south, or the West Coast
negroes, so many of whom populated
our Southern States.[23]

In comparing the different races of Africa, Dye
wrote:

The darker color and other lubricated
negro features seen generally among
the people of West and South Africa,
in contrast with a less glossy black
(and even lighter color), and
European features of the people
of further East and North Africa,

69

indicates, unmistakably, not only
the ethnic movement, but the
direction of the opposing streams.

Not unlike, but even more handsome,
more expressive are the features
of the Abyssinian than those of
the better known and more tranquil
Nubian. The latter, being without
mountains' shelter, have suffered
more abundantly, if not so frequently,
impregnation of negro blood flowing
down the Nile.[24]

When the American officers, Purdy, Colston, and
Mason were leading an expedition surveying in the
region between Bernice and Berber in Northern Sudan,
their Sudanese and Egyptian subordinates began to
purchase slaves. The slave trade was still flourishing
in that region despite the government's laws and
efforts to suppress it. Mason and Colston, being from
Virginia, had declared that the Negro was fit for
nothing for slavery.[25]

The following incident shows that the American
officers did not only keep a blind eye to their
subordinates' illegal activities, but openly condoned
them. A Coptic soldier purchased a young female
slave for eighty dollars, and claimed that he would
marry her upon his arrival in Cairo. On the way back,
the slave ran away on the grounds that her owner was
a Christian. However, the runaway slave was captured
in the desert and returned. The three officers held
a court for her trial, at which she claimed that she
ran away because her owner was beating her constantly.
Their verdict was to return her to her owner; and the
expedition proceeded.[26]

Whether officer Mason agreed with his two
colleagues, or just went along with them is not clear.
Mason was a graduate of Annapolis Naval Academy, who
worked in the Confederate fleet during the Civil War.
But in Egypt, he turned into an avowed anti-slavery
activist, a position that angered his superiors to
the extent that the Khedive himself intervened by
cable to block his appointment on the grounds that he
was not qualified or trustworthy, and directed the
Governor-General to review his decision.[27] But he
continued to hold the job for a few months, during

which time he explored the area between Dufile and Lake Albert. In 1878 he resigned from the Egyptian army and joined the Survey Department in Cairo. In the same year, he was appointed as chief of the anti-slave trade organization on the Red Sea coast. In 1884 he was appointed Governor of Musawaa.[28]

While all the American officers, Southerners and Northerners, performed their duties as disciplined soldiers within the bounds of their contracts, only Mason, and a Southerner for that matter, went beyond the call of duty to participate in the anti-slave trade movement in the Nile Valley. Either his position against the suppression of the slave trade changed after the Civil War, or he joined the Confederate Army for reasons other than the right of the South to possess slaves.

A more typical Southern officer was Charles Chaillé-Long, who was chosen by Gordon to become his chief-of-staff. He claimed in his memoirs that the Khedive had arranged an interview with him without Gordon's knowledge, for the purpose of monitoring Gordon's efforts in suppressing the slave trade. According to Chaillé-Long the Khedive informed him:

> You have been chosen as his (Gordon's) Chief of Staff for many reasons, chief of these, to guard the interests of the Egyptian government. An expedition is being organized in London under the command of a pseudo-American named Stanley, ostensibly to succour Dr. Livingston, but in reality to plant the British flag in Uganda. Go to Gondokoro, but lose no time in making your way to Uganda; anticipate the London expedition, make a treaty with the King of Uganda, and Egypt will owe you a debt of everlasting gratitude. Go and success attend you. Insha-lah.[29]

The Khedive was a shrewd man. He knew that Gordon was more inclined toward suppressing the slave trade than in geographical expansion. Although Gordon made the choice, the final word belonged to the Khedive.

His private interview with, and his approval of Chaillé-Long indicate that the Khedive had prior knowledge that the man was not committed to suppressing the slave trade. Indeed, Chaillé-Long's later actions showed where he stood.

After successfully carrying out his mission, Chaillé-Long wrote a long letter from Khartoum to the American Agent and Consul-General in Cairo highlighting his explorations in the Lakes region. He had discovered that Lake Victoria was larger than the figures given by the British explorer, Speke. He reported a new lake between Lakes Victoria and Albert, and that the Nile between Maudagui and Fewera was navigable. Finally he claimed to have established strong relations with Mutesa I, King of Uganda.[30]

While sojourning at Mutesa's court, Chaillé-Long was presented with an albino Negro boy. He said that Mutesa was in the habit of surprising him, and added:

> M'Tsee, a man who though ignorant
> has proper intelligence, struggles
> for light to a certain point (for
> you know, Mr. Consul, I am one of
> those who believe in the limited
> point to which the negro only can
> go). Our compatriot Fred D.
> is the son of a white gentleman in
> my state.[31]

Mutesa also presented him with one of his daughters, nine years old. Chaillé-Long accepted both children. On his way back from the Zandi land, bought a dancing pigmy female, named Tiki Tiki in exchange for a piece of red cloth. A tribal chief presented him with another. He brought all of them back to Khartoum, and used to refer to them as "my anthropological collection."[32] Chaillé-Long presented Tiki Tiki to the Khedive, who accepted her in turn, and occasionally introduced her to entertain his guests. Eventually she found her way to Vienna.[33]

In another incident, an American officer, Charles Iverson Graves, who was born in Georgia and graduated from the United States Naval Academy, refused to show respect to the Queen Mother's black eunuch. Graves was attending an official committee meeting when the eunuch entered. Everyone jumped to his feet in fear and respect for this most influential individual. Graves was taken by surprise, and joined the rest, but when the eunuch stood up to leave, and everyone did likewise, Graves refused to stand, a gesture that no doubt frightened the rest of the committee members for fear of reprisal.[34]

William Wing Loring, a former Confederate officer, wrote in his book, A Confederate Soldier in Egypt (1884), accusing Great Britain of contradicting its declared policy by allowing Gordon to legalize the slave trade in 1884. He claimed that the withdrawal of the Turco-Egyptian administration, in spite of its repression and injustice, would turn Khartoum into a great center for the slave trade.[35]

In order to understand the contradiction between the American officers' efforts to suppress the slave trade in accordance with the Egyptian government's policy, and their contempt for the Negro race, we have to consider their backgrounds and what was going on in the United States at the time. Abolition of slavery, in any slave society, did not preclude the existence of bias against the freed slaves and their offspring, especially if the slaves were of a different race, color, language and culture. At such times, bias is transformed into racism. In this respect, the attitudes of the American soldiers, especially those from the South, were no different from those of the Khedive Ismail, down to the humblest peasant or nomadic Northern Sudanese. All were products of slave societies.

THE UNION VS THE CONFEDERACY IN EGYPT

An interesting aspect of the American officers' experience in the Nile Valley was that of the relationship between those who fought with the Confederacy, and those who fought for the Union. Their compatriot, Judge Pierre Crabites, who wrote a book about their adventure claimed that they worked side by side in the Nile Valley, free of hatred.[36] Crabite's statement is contradicted by the feud between some of the Southern officers and George H. Butler, the American Agent and Consul-General (March 1870-July 1871) in Egypt, and one of President Grant's political appointees. His uncle was the famous Northerner, General Benjamin Butler, who at the time was a member of Congress from the state of Massachusetts.

From the start the new, rash and uncompromising Consul-General had drawn a line between Northern and Southern officers. He continued to refer to the latter group in his despatches as the "rebels." When General Mott, who recruited the other officers, and was the highest ranking American officer in Egypt, differed with his boss, Chahin Pasha, the Minister of War, he was removed from his job as the Egyptian army chief-of-staff, and given the honorary job of the Khedive's aide-de-camp. He was replaced by another American officer, General Charles Stone.

Butler wrote to the State Department, informing them that the British and French consuls-general in Egypt, who were against the employment of the American officers, were using this new appointment to arouse the jealousies of the Southern officers, as both Mott and Stone were Northerners. He added that

> There have been various reasons
> assigned for this act, but it
> results in truth from the machin-
> ation and intrigues of the
> ex-Confederate West Point officers
> from America, who objected to serve
> under an officer of the Union Army,
> and one who is not a graduate of
> the military Academy. These
> dissatisfied officers succeeded
> in entirely destroying the friendly
> relation that once existed between
> his excellency Chahin Pasha, the
> Minister of War, and General Mott.[37]

In another despatch Butler reported the promotion of Lieutenant-Colonel Purdy, a Northerner, saying:

> This is the first promotion made
> among the American officers. The
> Northern officers have without
> exception secured the good will and
> confidence of the Khedive's govern-
> ment. This was not true of the
> ex-Confederates as a rule--although
> many of them are esteemed as brave,
> competent and useful officers.[38]

Butler tried to persuade General Stone to promote Northern officers at the expense of Southern officers. Infuriated by Butler's interference, General Stone complained to the State Department. The Khedive Ismail intimated a similar complaint to the American Minister at Constantinople.[39]

In September of 1871, Butler informed the State Department that he had received application from the American officers for consular protection. Except for the Southern officers who graduated from West Point, he had permitted their registration as proteges. Revealingly, he reported:

> My official relations as well as
> private with these officers are
> of the pleasantest nature and it
> is at their request that I ask
> for your instructions as they are
> under the impression that being
> graduates of West Point and
> Annapolis, having held commission
> as generals (some of them) in
> the Confederate Service and not
> being pardoned, they are deprived
> of their rights.[40]

The response of the State Department was sharp and precise. It informed him that it was the duty of the American government to protect its citizens abroad without exception, in accordance with its international obligations and general laws. He was also informed that, to their knowledge, there was nothing against any of the American officers in Egypt.[41] A copy of General Stone's complaint against him was enclosed, and he was asked to respond. After denying Stone's allegation that he had sent a threatening message to the Khedive to increase the promotion of Union officers, he described Stone as:

> ...the Brigadier General Stone
> who lost the battle of Ball Bluff
> and was imprisoned for a long
> time on a charge of treason. He
> is now an avowed enemy of the
> United States and American interests
> in Egypt and has used his influ-
> ence to degrade or remove American
> officers to make way for Russians,
> Danes, and French.[42]

It is quite evident that the confrontation
between the Southern officers and the American Agent
and Consul-General had reached a point that might
revive the old hostility and hatred of the Civil War
in a foreign country. But for one reason or another
their confrontation did not touch the sensitive area
of slavery and the slave trade in the Nile Valley,
in the sense that the two parties to the confrontation
would trade accusations. One could assume that the
American officers and community had reached a
spontaneous and undiscussed gentlemen's agreement to
keep themselves out of such a situation. However,
the American newspapers accused Butler of being a
drunkard and of acquiring concubines.[43]

In July of 1872, Butler and a Northern officer
became involved in an argument with three Southern
officers that developed into a shooting spree. One
of the Southern officers was wounded. Butler cabled
his uncle, General Butler, through the State Department, saying: "Leave, immediately. Important. Rebel
officers attempted my assassination. One assassin
shot."[44] The State Department approved, and instructed
him that the person he left behind in charge of the
Consulate would not be allowed to perform any diplomatic functions.[45] He was relieved of his duties
while on his way to the United States, thus bringing
an end to a short, tumultous period in the history
of the American community in Egypt in the nineteenth
century.

One cannot help questioning the seriousness of
the Khedive Ismail in suppressing the slave trade in
the Nile Valley, while employing Southern officers
in his army. He could have satisfied his need by
recruiting strictly from the large body of qualified
Northern officers. The only vindication that can be
found for the Khedive's action is that the Southern
officers, like their Northern counterparts, had performed their duties with the same zeal and efficiency,
and had created no trouble for him with Baker and
Gordon, as far as the suppression of the slave trade
in the Nile Valley was concerned. As a matter of
fact, when compared to the Turco-Egyptian officials
in Egypt and Sudan, and most of them were military
men who were involved in the slave trade, the Southern
officers had not disgraced their country in this
regard.

PART TWO:

THE OFFICIAL RESPONSE

Chapter V

THE NILE VALLEY AND THE AMERICAN CIVIL WAR

American consular activities in the Nile Valley
were established in 1832, when the American Consular
Agency was opened in Alexandria. In 1835, it was
elevated to a consulate, and to a consulate-general in
1848. The first reference to the slave trade in the
consular despatches occurred as late as 1850. This
despatch to the Consulate-general mentioned that among
the annual reports from Jedda (Arabia) were one hundred
Ethiopian slaves. [1] The Consular-General made no
reply.

When Said Pasha, the Viceroy, imported one
thousand slaves from the Sudan to work as his special
guards, they were described by the Consul-General
thusly:

> One of the most striking of these was
> a troop of gigantic Nubians, clad
> from head to heel in the chain armour
> of the early Crusaders with their
> black barbs in like panoply, and a
> grim troop they looked, with their
> jet black faces, black barbs, roll-
> ing white eyes and rattling chain
> armour. [2]

The outbreak of the American Civil War in April
of 1861 was covered extensively by the British and
French press, and the Turco-Egyptian elites who read
these papers were aware of its causes and developments
from the start. When the Egyptian Foreign Minister
paid a courtesy visit to the new American Agent and
Consul-General in the same year, he expressed his wish
that the American government succeed in maintaining
the integrity and unity of the American soil. He also
expressed his admiration of the American government's
ability and preparedness to meet the challenge. [3]
Surprisingly, the subject of slavery and the slave trade
was not mentioned, unless such discussion had been
omitted from the Consular-General's report.

There was an irony in this diplomatic conspiracy
of silence, if such was the case. While the American
Consul-General was the representative of a government
waging a war in the name of abolishing slavery on its

soil, the Egyptian minister was representing a government reluctant for reasons of its own to take similar steps to abolish slavery within its domains, despite and because of vigorous outside pressures from Christian European nations. Both officials were painfully aware that the raising of the subject of slavery was a nonplus, unnecessary and embarrassing regardless of their respective government's positions and policies toward it. The bottom line was that both their countries were slave societies suffering from the stigma, and there was no pride to be drawn from that.

The Civil War created side effects which directly affected the relationship between the American and Egyptian governments. The United States' involvement in the Civil War underlined the interesting and little-known incident of the despatch of Sudanese troops for services with the French in Mexico. Furthermore, the Civil War provided Egypt with the opportunity to expand and develop the production of its long-staple cotton. Both had not a little bearing on the question of slavery and the slave trade in the Nile Valley. These became the subject matter of the diplomatic interaction between the United States and Egypt during the years of war.

THE COTTON BOOM IN EGYPT

The production of cotton had doubled in the Southern region of the United States by the 1850's. When the Civil War erupted, the Southern states hoped to gain the support of Great Britain and France who depended on American cotton. They also hoped to convince both countries that the division of the United States would remove from their way a strong competitor. But the seige of the Southern ports by the Union's fleet, the large amounts of stored cotton in Europe, the development of new sources of cotton in India and Egypt, and finally, the opposition of the British working class forestalled the Southern economic pressure plan. [4]

The Union government found itself forced to encourage Egypt to increase its production of cotton. The Secretary of State wrote to the Consul-General in Alexandria instructing him to accompany the Khedive to London and encourage him to obtain the necessary equipment for cultivating cotton, and to insulate him from Southern propaganda. [5]

The Egyptian government showed its support of the
Union in two matters. First it issued its orders to
the Alexandria port authorities "to exclude all vessels
bearing an unrecognized flag from the harbors of
Egypt." Second, American manufacturers were placed "on
an equal footing with those of Great Britain" in
obtaining Egyptian cotton. [6]

What is important for this study is the fact that
the prosperity that ensued as a result of the cotton
boom in Egypt enabled the upper and middle classes and
even peasants to acquire Circassian and black slaves,
thereby increasing the demand for slaves during those
years. The period following the cotton boom, 1866
to 1900, was one of economic stress and witnessed the
dispossession of the peasants of their lands for
failure to pay debts. These peasants flocked to the
cities in large numbers, providing cheap manual labor
for which slaves formerly had been acquired. This no
doubt hastened the decline in the demand for slaves,
and facilitated the abolition of the slave trade. [7]

The relations between the American and Egyptian
governments were strong enough during the years of
the Civil War for the Viceroy to offer to the Union
forces 47,357 new French Minie guns for sale. But
despite the Consul-General's eagerness to conclude the
transaction, the Americans declined politely on the
grounds that American guns were superior, and that
several orders had already been placed for them. [8]

These relations were soon strained with the dis-
patch by the Egyptian government of a Sudanese batta-
lion to fight with the French in Mexico. Evidently
the Egyptian government was unaware of the implications
of ·its action on American-Egyptian relations. In a
naive way it thought it was taking advantage of a
situation that presented itself at the right time, not
aware of the fact that the French government was mani-
pulating Egypt to serve its own interests.

SUDANESE SOLDIERS IN MEXICO

In his venture to install a monarchy in Mexico
with Maximillian I as Emperor, Napolean III sought
and obtained troops from Austria, Belgium, and Egypt.
He reached a verbal and secret agreement with
Viceroy Said Pasha in 1862 to provide him with a

"negro regiment" of one thousand five hundred soldiers.
It was assumed that they would be well-adapted to the
"hot and malarious plains inland of Vera Cruz."[9]
The agreement was not reduced to writing or made public for fear of antagonizing "the Turkish Sultan,
theoretically suzerain of Egypt, or Great Britain, the
guarantor of Turkish integrity."[10]

Said Pasha's decision to run the risk of such
action was based on three reasons: to gain the sympathy
of France in his struggle for independence, to test
the Sultan's seriousness in blocking such acts of independence, and to expose his troops to fighting a
modern war. It seems that Said Pasha, who was lured
into this situation by Napoleon III, was not aware of
the international implications of of his actions. His
death in January of 1863, a few days after the departure
of the soldiers, left his successor, Ismail Pasha, with
the burden of justifying them.

The French frigate La Siene arrived at Alexandria
on the first January, 1863, carrying 1,100 troops
bound for Cochin China. They were transferred by land
to the Red Sea, and the frigate remained idle in the
port. On January 6th and 7th it was provided with
supplies. On the latter day the police captured fifty
able-bodied "Negroes" from the streets of Alexandria
and together with 450 "black" soldiers were shipped
out on La Siene.

The American Consul-General in Egypt, William
Thayer, in his first despatch, hastily written on
January 9, 1863, wondered about the international
implications of the incident and added that "perhaps
also, in the same case, the alleged attempt of the
emperor of the French to introduce a regiment of free
black troops into a country contiguous to our slave-
holding states may be a subject of curiosity to our-
selves."[11]

On January 12th, the Consular-General sent a
private letter to William Seward, United States
Secretary of State, describing the incident of the
capture of the innocent blacks from the street and
the demonstration of their screaming relatives. He
said that these scenes recalled "the worst practices
of the African slave trade and constituted an outrage
on humanity against which all Christian powers would
be justified in remonstration." Significantly, he

added, "This is of course not the language I should use in my official capacity to the government here."[12]

More than any other document in the American official correspondence between the Consulate-General and Washington, this private letter brings to light two facts: first, the existence of clearcut, unwritten instructions to avoid discussing certain issues, and second, the double stand or hypocrisy of which policy that allowed American officials to discuss the slave trade in Egypt in private and to avoid it when talking to their Egyptian counterparts. It is to be remembered that the letter was written during the years of the Civil War.

When the Minister of Foreign Affairs visited the American Consulate-General, he denied that the Sultan knew beforehand about the black Sudanese regiment. He mentioned that the original request of Napoleon III was for one thousand and five hundred soldiers, but that Said decided to send only five hundred. Thayer informed the Minister that the number of troops was not at issue, but the principle of sending them, to which the Minister replied that when Said Pasha gave his acceptance, he was not aware of the international consequences, and that all he wanted was to do a favor for his friend, the French Emperor.

Thayer drew the Minister's attention to the fact that if the troops were sent by the Viceroy's order alone, that would be in violation of the Agreement of London of 1840 and the Porte's _Firman_ of 1841, by which Mohammed Ali's family was allowed to inherit the rule of Egypt and which specifically stated that the Viceroy had no right to make foreign policy decisions on his own. In such case, Thayer added, this would be the concern of the European powers that signed the Treaty and the Sultan, and that the United States would have nothing to do with it. But if the orders to send them came from the Sultan, that would amount to a declaration of war on Mexico, which would in turn violate the neutrality principle on the North American continent, to which the United States government was committed.

The Minister admitted that his government had made a mistake and hoped that it would be a lesson to it in the future. Thayer then raised the matter of the coercion of the Sudanese soldiers.

> In reply to the reports of inhumanity
> and kidnapping, His Excellency said
> they were mostly exaggerations.
> Mr. De Beamal, the French Consul-
> General, gives the same assurances,
> though in my judgment, these reports
> in some cases are well established.
> His Excellency did not think the
> total number transported exceeded
> five hundred.
>
> The honorable candor of these
> official declarations left little
> to be desired except the return
> of the unfortunate men who had
> been so nummarily expatriated
> against their will.[13]

When Thayer pressed the next day for an official response, he was told that the Sultan's telegrams had led the Egyptians to take the decision not to send any more troops to Mexico. Thayer declared in a following despatch that he had reliable information that France had informed Great Britain in advance, in regard to sending black troops, and that the only country that had protested this action was the United States.[14]

It is evident that Thayer wanted his government to continue its pressure in Paris, Constantinople, and Cairo in the hope that such pressure would lead to the return of the Sudanese troops, but he changed his mind for two reasons. The first was the death of Said Pasha on January 18th, and the succession of Ismail Pasha. The second and more important was that Secretary of State Seward was against involvement in any foreign adventure while the Civil War ensued.

Seward went to the extent of saying that his government had no objection to the presence of French troops in Mexico. His objection was to the use of force to change governments. As for Emperor Maximillian I, the United States would recognize his rule if he enjoyed the support of his subjects. Seward's sole interest was to ensure the French support of the Union and to block them from providing material or moral support to the Confederacy.[15]

As a result of Seward's position, the question of the black Sudanese soldiers in Mexico was muted until the end of the Civil War. Seward succeeded in giving the French government a good reason for not recognizing the Confederacy; at the same time, giving Maximillian I the occasion to accept the Confederacy's recognition of his government at a time when he was eager for any recognition. However, the American Consulate-General in Mexico's capital continued to function without the United States' recognition of Maximillian I.

After the Civil War, the Sudanese regiment would have been forgotten until its members had either been killed in battle, fallen sick of tropical disease, or deserted, had it not been for the fact that Ismail Pasha, in an effort to avoid his predecessor's secrecy, called the American Consul-General and informed him that he was sending nine hundred more black Sudanese troops to replace the first regiment. He informed Charles Hale, the new American Consul-General, that his motive was humanitarian: to relieve the first, and by now, homesick, regiment. He explained that the French government would pay the heavy expenses of transportation.

Despite Ismail Pasha's direct and friendly approach, Hale's was a frontal attack, suggesting that the United States could, in like manner, send Negro troops for service in Egypt "if the vicious principle of interference which supports the Empire of Mexico to which the Pasha lends his soldiers should at any time be used by us."[16] He added that such arguments could be used to deter the Egyptian government from sending more troops to Mexico because "...it would be very foolish for him to do anything more that mgiht have the effect to provoke an intervention of the United States against himself in some turn of Egyptian affairs."[17]

Hale concluded his despatch by informing his government that he had asked an American missionary traveling to the Sudan to provide him with any information of troop movement.

Secretary of State Seward's aggressive and moralistic response was a reversal of his earlier policy toward the subject. He wrote that the earlier despatch concerning the Sudanese troops had gone unnoticed by his government, which at the time was "occupied with a peculiar condition of purely domestic affairs, and with the foreign embarrassment which grew out of that condition." He continued by saying that since then slavery had been abolished in the United States, and that the attention of Congress and the President were now focused on the events in Mexico which threatened "free republication institutions on this continent, an object with which we are accustomed to connect the desired ultimate consequence of the abolition of every form of compulsory civil or military servitude in this hemisphere."[18] Hale was instructed to convey that message to the Egyptian government, and to inform them that the United States government had sent similar messages to Paris and Constantinople.

Seward's new policy, and especially his inference that the black Sudanese soldiers were mere slaves transported against their will, scared both Paris and Constantinople. The French government resented the American attempt to extend its "municipal laws to foreign countries."[19] But it was unable to withstand the heat of the accusation that slave soldiers were fighting under the French flag. In order to save face, the French government decided not to ask for any more black Sudanese soldiers, but to reserve the right to ask for them if the need arose.

The Egyptian government proved to be more intran-sigent. The aggressive diplomatic line of the Ameri-cans carried with it the implication that the Sudanese soldiers were either slaves or had been coerced into fighting a distant war. The French capitulation was to their credit; and Egyptian capitulation would have been tantamount to an affirmation that there were indeed slaves in its army, and that they were being sent abroad to participate in foreign wars.

The Egyptian government had not responded to the Ameican message by the end of October. By that time, according to Hale, the British government had protested through its Consul-General, Colonel Stanton, to the Viceroy against his sending Sudanese troops to Mexico. The British government took advantage of the situation and asked the Viceroy to fulfill his promises to abolish slavery. Hale attested to the British effort in this regard, saying:

> ...any slave who can manage to
> get before the British consul is
> sent with the dragoman of the
> consulate to the local courts where

his free papers are demanded and
accorded.   In this way, Mr. Reade,
British consul at Cairo and
Mr. Hauley, British consul at
Alexandria, have secured the
manumission of at least twenty
each...since I have been here.
In one instance, it was a slave
woman who had escapted from a
pacha's harem and flex to
Mr. Reade's house.[20]

The difference between the British and American diplomatic initiative was great.   Whereas the Americans
merely opposed the presence of foreign slave soldiers
in the New World, the British attacked the root of the
problem: slavery in the Nile Valley.

While Hale was waiting for the Egyptian government's response, he received a cable from the State
Department informing him that the French government
had made it clear that it was not interested in employing more Sudanese soldiers for the time being.[21]

Two weeks later, Hale sent a despatch saying that
he was still waiting for the Egyptian response.   He
added, however, that he had no doubt in his mind that
"the proposed deportation of negroes from Egypt for
military service in Mexico, has been abondoned."   He
went on to say that

> ...there is even some reason to
> believe that the trouble in the
> Soudan, which has been assigned
> in Paris as a reason for the
> abandonment of the expedition,
> was caused, if not wholly, at
> least in part, by the destesta-
> tion entertained by the people,
> and especially among the men
> enrolled for military duty, for
> the distant service to which
> it was feared they were to be
> sent.[22]

The trouble to which Hale was referring was the
revolt which had broken out in the Fourth Regiment at
Kassala in Sudan.   This regiment was comprised of black
Jihadiyya (irregulars).   Even among the Egyptian and

87

Northern Sudanese soldiers and irregulars, they were
referred to as "black Jihadiyya." As soldiers in the
army, there were not slaves, but they were captured as
slaves or obtained from Nortern tribes in lieu of taxes.
Nevertheless, the stigma of slavery was always attached.
They were mainly drawn from the non-Muslim, racially
mixed tribes and their offspring of Southern Sudan and
Southern Darfur and Kordofan.[23]

The main reasons given for their revolt were the
six-month arrears in their salaries, and the arrogance
and cruel treatment of their Turkish and Egyptian officers. The underlying cause was the tensions created
by the discrepancy between their position as soldiers
and their status in a slave society. Interestingly
enough, the United States had been witnessing similar
revolts among its black troops after the Civil War for
similar reasons.

When the black Jihadiyya were ordered to prepare
for an expedition, they insisted on receiving their
arrear salaries. Their commander was outraged, and
resorted to force. The revolt broke out, and the
army and city were polarized. In essence, it became
a racial confrontation.[24] Thus the black Sudanese
troops who were prepared to be sent to Mexico to fight
under the French flag to suppress the Mexican revolution, carried on their own rebellion in the Sudan.
Their rebellion added to an already complicated international situation.

On November 16, 1865, the Egyptian Minister of
Foreign Affairs had an interview with Consular-General
Hale, and informed him that the Egyptian government was
determined to send the troops to Mexico. He wanted to
assure the American government that the number of
soldiers would not exceed the number of the first regiment, and that they were not slaves. In response,
Hale said that it was not clear whether the new regiment would be added to or would replace the first one,
as the Viceroy had indicated earlier. As for his
assurance that they were not slaves, Hale told the
Egyptian Minister that this did not answer the American
objection to the principle of sending foreign troops
to Mexico.

The Minister, Sherif Pasha, after hearing this
reply, claimed that, "This put an entirely new face
upon the affair, and could scarcely discredit the

accuracy of my information." Yet, in his reply to the Consul-General's first note on the subject, Sherif Pasha had heatedly denied the existence of slavery in Egypt, and explicitly stated that the Sudanese troops were not slaves, saying:

> Thus in the opinion of the cabinet of Washington, the Egyptian soldiers who make part of the French expedition to Mexico are to be regarded as slaves, and their stay there as contradicting the great measure of humanity which has freed all their brethren in America.
>
> Permit, Sir, to protest on my side, against the expression of an error so clear. Slavery no longer exists in Egypt. It was abolished there long before it was abolished in the United States, by the many sacrifices and glorious efforts on the part of the defenders of the Union. The negroes in the Egyptian territory are subject of His Highness by the same title and with the same rights as the other natives of the country. In serving under our flag they obey a law of conscription equal for all...This is not all. In virtue of a principle made applicable as long ago as the reign of our illustrious Mehemet Ali, all slaves enrolled under the flag became free in full right.[25]

The State Department's comments on Sherif Pasha's reply was that the French government had reiterated its assurances that it was against bringing any more Black Sudanese soldiers to Mexico. The American president, Hale was told, recommended to accept the French assurances and to discontinue discussion with the Egyptian government on the subject, unless France changed its mind. At such time, Hale was instructed to convey to the Egyptian government the message that, "In the opinion of the President, Negroes, natives of Africa, cannot rightfully be employed as soldiers in any way to subvert established political institutions, or disturb society on the American continent."[26]

He was instructed to contact directly his colleagues in Paris and Constantinople in case of emergency.

The crisis was resolved when a new government took over in Egypt on January 17, 1866. Nubar Pasha became the Minister of Foreign Affairs, described by Hale as a "Christian (Armenian) and has always believed to have a leaning to English rather than French predilections in Egypt."[27]

In an interview with Hale, Nubar Pasha promised to send a memorandum to him as soon as he obtained the consent of the Viceroy, containing the assurance that no more troops would be sent to Mexico. "He made no attempt to conceal the fact that he has always disliked the Mexican expedition," said Hale.[28]

In May of 1867 the first black Sudanese regiment returned from Mexico after a four and a half-year absence. On their return home, they stopped in Paris, where they were received by the Emperor, who bestowed upon them medals of honor. They were received by the Khedive (new title of Viceroy), where they were equally honored. According to the Egyptian government newspaper, the number of the regiment was originally 447, led by two officers and a translater, of whom 126 died.

In spite of the fact that historians have carefully studied the political and diplomatic side of the crisis raised by the presence of the black Sudanese troops in Mexico and the motives of Napolean III, Said Pasha and Ismail Pasha, they overlooked the fact that the crisis intertwined with the institution of slavery in the Nile Valley. They also overlooked the fact that American diplomacy under William Seward had used the slavery issue to achieve one limited goal, and that was to exclude European involvement in the affairs of the New World. He reduced the issue of abolition of the slave trade and slavery in the Nile Valley from a moral issue to a concrete and limited political situation. Seward's moralistic argument against slavery and the forced employment of African slaves was no more than a tactic to scare the French. Once he achieved his objective of scaring the proud descendants of those who fomented the French Revolution, he washed his hands of the whole subject. His country was already suffering from the heritage of slavery, in spite of its abolition.

Chapter VI

FROM INDIFFERENCE TO PROCRASTINATION

During the years of the Civil War and immediately thereafter, the relations between the United States and Egypt, as far as the issue of slavery and the slave trade in the Nile Valley were concerned, were typified by indifference. In spite of the efforts of the various American consulars-general in Egypt to involve their government in the matter, Washington remained aloof, concerning itself only with the political issues that might affect the outcome of the War, and later, Reconstruction. By the end of Reconstruction, the question of slavery and the slave trade had become an ordeal to be forgotten, especially in the distant region of the Nile Valley.

WILLIAM THAYER, AMERICAN CONSUL-GENERAL, ALEXANDRIA (1861-1863)

In his address to the Consular Corps, upon his succession as Viceroy in January of 1863, Ismail Pasha spelled out the main features of his plan to modernize Egypt. He stressed the need to develop agriculture and commerce; the suppression of government corvée (forced labor for public works) which had withdrawn so much labor from agriculture; spread of public education; strict administration of justice; and order and economy in government expenditure.[1] No mention was made of the abolition of slavery and the slave trade in the Nile Valley.

In his despatch concerning the reception and the Viceroy's address, William Thayer, the American Agent and Consul-General, failed to report the fact that the subject of slavery and the slave trade had not been part of the Viceroy's address, in spite of the fact that only nine days earlier he had sent a twenty-page despatch describing "the clandestine embarkation" of black Sudanese soldiers to Mexico and his vehement protest against that. Moreover, less than one month prior to the Viceroy's address, President Lincoln had issued the Emancipation Proclamation in the midst of the raging Civil War.

At the same reception, the French Consul-General had asked the Viceroy forthwith whether the abolition of the corvée would affect the work on the Suez Canal, which was largely carried on by that system. The Viceroy denied that it would. The French Consul-General was quick to interrupt the Viceroy when he thought that French interests were threatened. Likewise, it was incumbent upon the American Consul-General to see the relationship between the corvee and the slave trade in the Nile Valley, and the newly-issued Emancipation Proclamation in the United States, and to express his government's support of the termination of the corvee if not the slave trade. The absence of such a reference, at such a time in the history of the United States and the history of relations between Egypt and the United States, is indicative of the fact that in the minds of the consular representatives there was not association between what was happening in the two countries; and furthermore, that there was no moral position toward the question of slavery in the Nile Valley.

If such was the case with the American and Egyptian officials, it was not so for the ruling class in Egypt. A heated debate which ensued between Prince Halim Pasha, the second in line for succession, and Thayer was indicative of the difference between the two attitudes.* In his argument, Thayer admitted of racial discrimination in the United States, and blamed it on the resentment of the new, ignorant immigrants from Europe. The Prince claimed that a slave could marry the daughter of his master, and tried to justify the existence of slavery by the absence of democratic institutions. Both the Prince and the American Consul-General were the products of slave societies, in which African slavery constituted an integral part of the social structure. Their reluctant admissions and evasive justifications indicate that they were aware of the immorality of slavery and the slave trade. Instead of developing a combined stance against, or strategy to attack the institution of slavery in the Nile Valley, the two were bogged down in a high school debate that robbed the subject of its moral content and responsibility.

Thayer concluded that despatch by apologizing for the length of it and hoped it would not be considered

* See Appendix A

irrelevant. This happened at a time when the Civil War was at its height.[2]

In a following despatch, he complained of the ignorance of the Egyptian officials of the history and political development of the United States. He referred to their failure to take a moral stand vis a vis the Civil War was an example of their ignorance. Because most of them knew the French language, Thayer distributed among them copies of Bigelow's book about the United States.[3]

Between the sudden death of Thayer in August of 1863, and the arrival of his successor, Charles Hale in August of 1864, the relations between Egypt and the United States deteriorated to the point of disruption. The acting Consul-General had intervened to protect a protege who had got into trouble with the police. He subsequently lowered the United States flag, and called for sending a frigate to show American muscle, which request was ignored.[4]

CHARLES HALE, AMERICAN CONSUL-GENERAL, ALEXANDRIA (1864-1870)

Taking advantage of a social gathering of the Consular Corps and top Egyptian officials, Charles Hale praised the Viceroy for the progress of Egypt. He surmised that "no doubt the present extraordinary prosperity of Egypt may be attributed to a large degree to the American war, but our war is undertaken in the cause of humanity." He expressed his satisfaction and pleasure that a friendly country like Egypt would reap such incidental benefits.[5]

Hale's remarks were widely reported in the Egyptian press, and a few days later, the Viceroy Ismail Pasha expressed to him his gratification. Hale reported to his government:

> The Pacha in allusion to the grandeur of our war, and its probable results in the extinction of slavery, described to me in detail his efforts for the amelioration of the conditions of the laborers in Egypt and for the promotion of agricultural prosperity.[6]

Ismail's statement is rather intriguing. He began
by praising the United States government for abolishing
slavery and, in apparent comparison, spoke of his
efforts to aid the Egyptian laborer, as if assuming
that there was no slavery in Egypt and the Sudan or
that such was not part of his concern. More interesting
than the Pasha's evasiveness was the fact that Hale
did not comment on the Pasha's statement and its
inconsistency.

After the end of the Civil War, Hale had a long
interview with Ismail Pasha, who told him that the
defeat of the Confederacy had helped him in purchasing
from Great Britain two frigates and a factory for
producing small weapons that were originally made for
the Confederacy. On the other hand, the end of the
war had produced a fall in the prices of cotton from
which resulted a financial crisis. The landowners
and fellaheen were expected to suffer the most.
According to Hale, the government was planning to make
available loans for both to meet their needs.[7]

The Emancipation Proclamation and the end of the
Civil War, with the defeat of the Southern states,
had given the United States an image of the protector
of freedom and democracy. It also put upon her the
burden of defending these noble principles, at least
in the eyes of the rest of the world. For instance,
the American Mission intervened on behalf of a Miss
Alexina Finnie, to the American Consul-General to put
some of her Sudanese attendants under the protection
of the American consulate-general.[8] At first the
Reverend Gulian Lansing of the United Presbyterian
Church contacted Hale, and discussed the subject with
him. Early in September of 1865, he made an official
application. Hale sent the application and letter
of Miss Finnie to the State Department, recommending
that the seven young Sudanese be granted American
protection as proteges. He said:

> In her solitary position in the
> Upper country, she naturally
> gathered about her, with their full
> consent, a small body of black
> attendants. Having a very exact
> understanding of the usages of
> the country, in order that there
> might be no possible mistake
> about the status of these blacks,

she took them before the magistrate
of the first principal town which
she entered within the Egyptian
frontier, where she tendered them
permission and means to return;
these they declined, and their declaration in open court of eager
willingness to accompany her of
their own free will was recorded.

Upon her arrival at Cairo, Miss Finnie placed her
"little family of blacks" at the American Mission's
school

> ...where she pays the whole expense
> of their maintenance and tuition.
> It may be remarked that these
> blacks, fresh from the banks of the
> White Nile, in the torrid zone of
> Africa, evince a remarkable apti-
> tude for learning and were able
> to read a few months after entering
> the school.

Hale then proceeded to shed light on the status
of black Sudanese in Egypt at the time:

> These negroes are neither Ottoman
> nor Egyptian subjects. They cannot
> live safely in Egypt without the
> protection of some Frank power.
> In saying this, I do not impugn the
> justice of His Highness the Pacha,
> but I state a fact arising from
> the peculiar administration here;
> unless it is known to government
> officials, especially those of low
> office, the people in such condition
> have a protecting power behind
> their rights, they are liable to
> become a prey to oppression in their
> persons, and to seizure of their
> property, if they have any.

Hale explained that European consulates-general
put any number of proteges under their protection, a
practice that was accepted as a matter of course.
But he lamented that he was unable to offer them
protection because of previous restrictions from the

State Department, limiting this practice to American citizens and employees of the consulate-general and its consular agencies.[9]

Finally, Hale concluded his lengthy despatch with the following:

> The reasons why this application is made to me, rather than the representative of any other power, will readily occur to you, as well as the reasons why it would be difficult to refuse it, in view of the superb position which our country at this moment occupies in the face of the world, with reference to slavery and the negro race. I take this opportunity to mention that the British consulate is frequently called upon to exercise its good offices in releasing from slavery some poor wretches from the upper country....His Highness the Pacha takes no exception to such interference; indeed, he professes to welcome it, as illustrating his good will; but it is certain that without such interference in such cases, his benevolent professions would be unavailing.[10]

Hale had stopped short of asking openly for the lifting of restrictions placed on the American Consul-General by the State Department so that he could proceed like his British counterpart in obtaining freedom papers for slaves. Yet the response of the State Department ignored his implied request. The response was: "The President has instructed me to inform you that he regards this case as exceptional, but not to be drawn into precedent. Your proposition in relation thereto is therefore approved."[11] Thus the President of the United States had firmly blocked any chance of his country shouldering any moral responsibility for helping those slaves who had the courage and desire to obtain their freedom by taking advantage of this loophole. This, at a time when the British were exploiting it to the maximum.

The next entanglement of the United States government in the question of slavery and the slave trade in the Nile Valley came from an unexpected quarter, Cuba. The American Consul-General in Havana, General Torbert, sent a despatch on June of 1872 calling the attention of the State Department to an item of news that appeared in the city's newspaper, Diario de la Marina, in regard to importing into Cuba contracted laborers from Egypt and Abyssinia "which means nothing more than slavery." He reported:

> In this connection I can only say at present that there is a report in the city that there has been two cargoes of negroes landed in the bay or district of Guantanamo. One, it is said, for Don Antonio Baro of this city, probably the largest producer in the island and who has plantations in that part of the island. The other, it is said for the firm of Polledo Co. at Matauras.
>
> It is difficult, almost impossible, to get hold of any positive evidence in the matter. I have been informed by parties considered reliable, but they will not allow their names to be used.
>
> The English and Austrian Consuls-General have been told the same thing and I can safely say that it is generally believed. I have written to the Consuls and Agent in that district to use every means in their power to try and find out the truth or falsity of the report.[12]

The newspaper mentioned that Don Enselrio Soler of Havana, at the time residing at Barcelona, had solicited permission from the Colonial Ministry to introduce into the Island of Cuba "hired colonists" from Egypt and Abyssinia. The paper added that his petition had been referred to the Superior Civil Governor of that Island, for information concerning the particulars of the petition, after hearing the report of the Central Committee of Colonization created by his authority.

The Acting Secretary of State at the time was
Charles Hale, the former Agent and Consul-General
to Egypt (1864-1870). His response was prompt. He
relayed a copy of General Torbert's despatch and a
translation of the newspaper article to the American
Consul-General in Egypt, instructing him thusly:
"Although the report of the Diario is not credited
here, nevertheless, it is desirable to ascertain the
facts in the case. You are consequently instructed
to make inquiries in the proper quarter and to report
the result to this department.[13]

One week later, Hale fired off another instruction
to the Consul-General in Egypt, informing him that he
had received another despatch, dated July 2nd, from
General Torbert, containing a contradiction of his
earlier report; and that "it is therefore not necessary
that you should proceed further in the matter."[14]

It is not clear what the United States government
would have done had General Torbert's and the paper's
reports been correct. Judging from its position
concerning the despatching of the black Sudanese
regiment to Mexico in 1865, perhaps no steps would have
been taken to interfere with the existing slavery and
slave trade in the Nile Valley. Any action would have
been limited to diplomatic protests to Egypt and
Cuba, asking for the prohibition of the importation
of African slaves to the New World.

RICHARD BEARDSLEY, AMERICAN CONSUL-GENERAL,
ALEXANDRIA (JULY 1872 - DECEMBER 1875)

In December of 1872, the New American Consul-
General, Richard Beardsley, sent a despatch concerning
a conversation he had had with Khedive Ismail on the
occasion of presenting the American Consul to him
at Port Said. The Khedive was evidently upset by
the tidings from Baker's expedition. Baker had,
according to the Khedive, penetrated into Equatoria
with three hundred soldiers, probably to suppress
the slave trade. In the Khedive's opinion, the
expedition was a failure, and Baker had not confined
himself to the letter or spirit of his instructions.

In Beardsley's judgment:

> Evidently His Highness is much
> displeased with Sir Samuel Baker
> and I presume he is especially
> annoyed that commerce with the
> headwaters of the Nile has been
> for the moment interrupted. He
> seems to think that Sir Samuel
> is himself to blame for many of
> his difficulties....It will not
> do to condemn Sir Samuel unheard.
> It cannot be denied that his
> mission is a most difficult one,
> the fruits of which even if suc-
> cessful, may not be immediately
> apparent. If His Highness
> earnestly desires the suppression
> of the slave trade he must expect
> a temporary derangement of the
> commerce with the slave trading
> communities which he must be
> satisfied to accept as a present
> evil for the sake of a future
> good.[15]

Unlike his predecessor, George Butler, the new Consul-General was not embroiled in personal feuds with the American community, and had ample time to follow the political developments in Egypt and Sudan. His despatch relating his conversation with the Khedive was the first detailed and well-informed account of the Sudan, and the slave trade in Egypt's southern provinces.

One day later, he sent another despatch which covered certain aspects of his talk with the Khedive which was not discussed in the previous despatch. The Khedive had expressed satisfaction with the rail-ways system in Lower Egypt, and a desire to extend the same to Upper Egypt and Sudan. According to Beardsley, the Khedive thought Egypt's mission was "to civilize Africa by pushing up through the valley of the Nile and overflowing Nubia and the Sudan. To do this the railways system of Upper Egypt must be completed and communication established with those countries."[16] The Khedive was determined to connect Egypt, Sudan, the Territory of Bogos, which he claimed was Egyptian, and the port of Massawa with systems of land and water transportation.

Beardley's concern with the political developments in Egypt, and his extensive coverage of them was unprecedented. When the London papers published a report that the Khedive was sending an expedition of 5,000 soldiers under the pretext of assisting Livingston in his exploration, but in fact, to invade Abyssinia, Beardsley contacted Sherif Pasha for explanation. Sherif Pasha told him that the expedition was comprised of only one hundred men, under the American officer, Purdy Bey; that it was intended for the rescue of Sir Samuel Baker, and as the Nile above Khartoum was unnavigable, the expedition would probably reach him by way of Zanzibar.[17]

When Sir Barth Frere, the British anti-slavery representative, came to Egypt, Beardsley mentioned in a report that Frere's destination was Zanzibar, to discuss the suppression of the slave trade with its Sultan. He reported:

> Sir Barth had several interviews with the Khedive and was very active in procuring all possible information concerning the slave trade in Egypt. The general result of his opinions may be inferred from his remark that he had not expected that his work was to begin in Egypt.

> I think he left Egypt with the feeling that it will be difficult to suppress the slave trade in Central Africa while the demand for slaves in Egypt remains as great as at present.

> I hope to be able to send you some statistics on this subject which will throw some light on the much debated question as to the actual extent of slavery in Egypt.[18]

In February of 1873, Beardsley sent a report on the proposed railway to the Sudan, written by Sir John Fowler, the British civil engineer who was appointed consulting engineer for the Egyptian government in 1871. Echoes of the anti-slavery movement were rife within the lengthy despatch:

This work cannot but be of great
national benefit in developing and
utilizing a vast and fertile country
which is now comparatively worthless.
The Soudan and the country within
reach of the navigable waters of
the Nile, is capable of great development, and is rich in many
things which Egypt needs. The soil
is said to be well adapted to the
growth of cotton, grain, and sugar,
timber is comparatively plentiful,
labor is abundant and cheap and it
is hoped that coal may be found
within reasonable distance of the
Nile. Nothing will contribute
more powerfully to demoralize and
destroy the slave trade in Soudan
than the railway, and in that point
of view alone it is a desirable and
praiseworthy enterprise.[19]

The short stay of Sir Barth Frere had evidently
influenced Beardsley, who was already inclined against
the traffic. His active coverage had aroused the
interest of the Department of State, which was not well
acquainted with the political developments in the Nile
Valley. The response to his conversation with the
Khedive Ismail concerning Baker called into question
the sincerity of the Khedive in his efforts to suppress
the slave trade:

There is more or less of mystery
about the expedition of Sir Samuel
Baker which the despatches from
your Consulate do not enable the
Department to solve. From his
nationality and antecedents, it
can scarcely be supposed that he
would undertake any expedition for
the purpose of promoting the slave
trade. It is understood, however,
that the Khedive is not interested
in and certainly not zealous in
the suppression of that traffic,
although Sir Samuel is nominally
at least in his service.

As to the expedition that Purdy Bey was to lead for the relief of Baker, the State Department thought it incredible that any expedition for the relief of Baker should proceed by way of Zanzibar; and that "if Purdy should take that course, he must have some other object and possibly it may be to encourage the Sultan of Zanzibar to keep up the slave trade, which this government and that of Great Britain have recently endeavored to induce him to suppress. You will be diligent in collecting and reporting information on this interesting subject."[20]

In response to the State Department's memorandum, Beardsley said that the mystery about Baker's mission was as great in Egypt as in Europe. He concluded, however, that:

> Baker's original instructions will probably never be known unless he lives to tell them himself, but it is beyond question that the chief object of the expedition was to bring within the pale of Egyptian rule and authority, the country bordering on the White Nile and the Great Lakes, to establish a regular and safe line of communication between those regions and Egypt proper; to encourage agriculture and commerce, and to destroy the slave trade. From what the Khedive has informed me at different times, I am satisfied that he expected Baker to regard the destruction of the slave trade as a matter of secondary importance which would follow from the subjugation of the country. His mission was to conciliate the tribes and to disturb the commerce and trade with the Lower Nile as little as possible.

Beardsley additionally reported that Baker attached more importance to suppressing the slave trade, counted too much on the Egyptian troops with him, and expected too much from the Khedive's promises. He also referred to a rumor about an understanding between the Khedive and the Sultan of Zanzibar to defeat the mission of Sir Barth Frere.[21]

It seems that the State Department's letter, especially its reference to the role that the United States, along with Great Britain, had pledged to induce the Sultan to suppress the slave trade, and that part which instructed him to collect information, encouraged Beardsley to step up his coverage and concern.

In May of 1873, he sent a questionnaire of twenty-three items to the American Consular Agencies.[22] His objective was to collect information about the subject of slavery, the administration of justice in the provinces, and the conditions of the lower classes, among other things. He concluded his cover letter with the following: "With the approval of the Department I propose to issue a circular to all of the United States Consular Agents, prohibiting them from holding slaves or persons to involuntary servitude.[23]

Questions twenty-two and twenty-three read as follows:

> 22. Does slavery exist in your district to any great extent? Are there any public or private slave markets? How much is a good male slave worth and how much is a good female slave worth? How many slaves do you think are owned in your district? Where are they brought from? Do they ever demand their freedom and can they obtain it? Are they often punished and abused or are they generally well treated? How many slaves do you own and where did you obtain them?

> 23. Where and by whom are eunuchs manufactured? How much is a good eunuch worth and are there many in your district?

It is to be remembered that the American Mission had prohibited its members from owning slaves. It is also relevant to mention that the British has suppressed their vice-consulate in Khartoum in 1864 because their vice-consul, John Petherick, had been accused of engaging in the slave trade.[24]

Hamilton Fish, the Secretary of State, responded unfavorably to the circular, citing two reasons, the first being that Egyptians might not share in the opinion on the subject of slavery which prevailed in the United States and the West; and secondly, that the holding of slaves did not disqualify the holder for employment under the Egyptian government, and "having this sanction before them, it may be questioned whether your order or prohibition would meet with the submission which it is desirable should be observed by subordinates to their superior officers, especially in the case of Christian officers in a Mohammedan country." He did recommend, however, that preference be given to non-slave holders in nominations as Consular Agents; and if "the knowledge that such is the policy of this government will lead to discountenancing the holding of slaves, you will not hesitate to proclaim the intention of the government in that respect." Nevertheless, he considered it unadvisable to "cancel the commission of a good officer merely because he owns slaves in a country where such property is recognized, unless you can secure the appointment of a good officer who will abstain from the odious and barbaric traffic and ownership."[25]

Thus the initiative to salvage the passive position of American officialdom toward slavery in the Nile Valley was nipped in the bud. As long as a consular employee of the United States in the Nile Valley, whether American or Egyptian, was efficient, he was free to own slaves, concubines, and even eunuchs. Fish could have, like any chief executive, exercised the royal prerogative of ignoring embarrassing queries by troublesome subordinates, which would be understood to mean 'forget it.' But when he committed his reply to writing, at that time, he was stating official government policy.

Despite the State Department's rebuff of his initiative, Beardsley continued to press the State Department from different directions. From his parlance and argument, Beardsley was a devoted anti-slavery proponent. He served in Egypt at a time when the pressure of the British Anti-Slavery Society was at its apex, and when the Khedive Ismail was expanding his empire southward in the areas which were traditionally the source of African slaves for the Nile Valley. Between 1870 and 1874, the Egyptian administration was established in Southern Sudan; the area between

104

Gondokoro and the Great Lakes was nebulously annexed to Egypt, and finally Darfur was occupied and annexed. It should be remembered that the Egyptian geographical expansion occurred in the period when European interests in Africa were rising.

In September of 1873, Beardsley reported in regard to the intervention of the British consulate in freeing slaves who came there seeking freedom papers.[26] He wrote that the interception by the British consular authority had helped 1700 slaves to obtain their papers; and that without its interception, police officers would have turned them back to their masters.

Beardsley further reported that a treaty to suppress the slave trade was being negotiated between Egypt and Great Britain, its general features being to end slavery in five years; to make it a crime to buy or sell slaves after that time; and to make it a crime to make a eunuch. He concluded his despatch by saying optimistically:

> It will thus seem that the slavery question in Egypt is in a fair way of being satisfactorily and per-mantly disposed of. It is not to be supposed that the prospect is an agreeable one for His Highness the Khedive subjects, and even His Highness himself, might be excused for regretting the necessity of such a step in view of the immense advantage slavery would give him, for the moment, in his development of the Sudan and the Lake region.[27]

Beardsley's despatch concerning the British efforts to end the slave trade, by helping interested slaves obtain their freedom papers, and by negotiating a treaty, aroused a temporary interest in Hamilton Fish, who wrote:

> It would have been acceptable information to have learnt, if such practice obtained and the freedom of a slave could be procured through the imposition of a Consul or a Consular Agent, that the practice had not been confined to British

> Consuls. I cannot doubt, that
> American Consuls and Consular
> Agents would have shared in the
> laudable practice had they known
> that they might so easily have
> contributed to removing the
> shackles of slavery and set a
> fellow man at liberty.
>
> Should the treaty which you mention
> as likely to be negotiated between
> Egypt and Great Britain be carried
> into effect and be enforced it
> will be creditable to both govern-
> ments.[28]

Again, Fish succeeded in avoiding the basic issue.
What Beardsley was aiming at was to persuade his government to issue clear-cut instructions to help slaves
to obtain their freedom papers, and to lift its
restrictions on extending protection or protege status.
Instead, Fish attempted to question the accuracy of
Beardsley's statement, and to dubiously shift the
responsibility and burden to the helpless consuls.

Finally, Beardsley attacked the subject directly.
He wrote a despatch about slavery in Egypt, describing
it as being mild compared to other kinds known in
other parts of the world. He referred to Nubar Pasha's
letter to the British Consul at Mansoura in which
he tried to defend slavery in the Nile Valley as being
sanctioned by religion and the tradition of centuries;
and he enclosed a copy of Nubar Pasha's letter with
his despatch. Apparently Beardsley was in contact
with the British Consular officials in Egypt, and
his efforts to persuade his government to contribute
her share in suppressing the slave trade were coordin-
ated and concerted directly or indirectly with those
of his British friends.

He concluded this despatch with the first direct
and open appeal to the State Department to partake
in the pressure exerted on the Egyptian government
to end the slave trade, saying:

> In view of the present state of
> the negotiations on this subject
> would it not be for our govern-
> ment to represent to the Khedive

the great interest which it takes
in this matter to assure his
Highness that an energetic and
honest crusade against the slave
trade, on his part, will meet the
warm approval of the United
States.[29]

As for Fish's inquiry about the role played by
the American Consul-General and his subordinates in
securing freedom papers for slaves, Beardsley replied
that "the consular representatives of the United
States appeared to have exercised their authority in
favor of the liberation of slaves on various isolated
occasions in the past, but as a rule have been careful
not to make themselves conspicuous in this respect
owing to the fact that such action is liable to
subject them to the ill will of the local authorities."
He pointed out their lack of instructions on the
subject, and that although they had never refused to
assist slaves to obtain their freedom when applied
to for that purpose, they were rarely applied to for
the reason that it was the "general belief among
the slaves that the English consular Agents are
especially empowered to effect their release from
bondage."[30]

In this despatch, Beardsley had gone as far as a
subordinate could go in addressing his superior policy-
makers. His message was louder and clearer than ever.
There was no response from the State Department.

The appointment of Colonel Gordon to succeed Baker
as Governor of Equatoria started a new period in the
Egyptian government in the question of suppressing
the slave trade, a change that Beardsley observed and
reported in his despatch concerning the departure of
Gordon for the Sudan.

It is believed that he (Gordon)
will quietly carry out the views
of annexation and organization of
His Highness the Khedive without
manifesting undue zeal in the
suppression of the slave trade and
that his policy will be one of
conciliation so far as is consis-
tent with the objects of his
mission.

I hope to be able to report from
time to time on the progress of
the expedition and its important
work.[31]

In June of 1874, Beardsley reported the arrival
of Gordon in Gondokoro, and the orders he issued,
declaring ivory to be the government's monopoly,
forbidding entrance into Equatorial provinces without
a pass from a competent authority, and forbidding
recruitment of organized bands and importation of
firearms.[32]

After his return from his summer vacation in
Europe, he wrote, hailing the conquest of Darfur in the
most glowing anti-slavery rhetoric:

The Khedive is determined to
suppress the slave trade and
among the tribes further south
and the annexation of Darfour
is an important step in that
direction. It is proposed to
place the people of Darfour on
the same footing with Egyptians.
All natives held in bondage will
be liberated and all slaves who
have been bought from the neigh-
boring tribes within a certain
time will be sent back to their
respective countries. A vast
fertile region abounding in many
of the resources of wealth had
for many years been desolated
by the horrible traffic in human
flesh. It is a matter of vital
importance to those countries
themselves, as well as to the
commerce and prosperity of Egypt,
that the slave trade should be
suppressed and the energies
of the people directed into the
natural and legitimate channels
of agriculture and commerce.[33]

Beardsley's optimism about the intention of the
Khedive and the consequences of conquering Darfur and
annexing it to the Egyptian empire was not shared by

his more skeptical friends in the British Anti-Slavery Society, or by his compatriot, Colonel Purdy.[34]

Subsequent despatches of Beardsley expressed his confidence in Gordon's efforts:

> The slave trade in these parts appears to be for the moment at least, officially suppressed, and effective measure are being taken to open up a legitimate commerce with the negro tribes....Gordon's good sense is now helping to make things work, but should he be compelled to leave because of sickness or other causes things will return to old days.[35]

On January 23, 1876, Richard Beardsley died in Cairo. His death brought to an end a very important period of American consular concern, at least as far as keeping Washington informed and exposed.

Chapter VII

ELBERT ELI FARMAN, AMERICAN CONSUL-GENERAL
IN CAIRO, 1876-1881

Elbert E. Farman, United States Consul-General in Cairo, 1876-1881, arrived in Egypt during one of its most difficult periods. Since 1875, an Anglo-French Commission had been in control of the country's finances; and the British and French comptrollers were in constant disagreement with the embattled Khedive.

From the start, Farman resented the British and French interference in the affairs of Egypt. This resentment was further aggravated by their opposition to the acquisition of the obelisk, "Cleopatra's Needle" by the city of New York. As a result, Farman began to feel sympathetic towards the Khedive Ismail-- a sympathy that developed into admiration and advocacy of the Egyptian cause.

The Secretary of State at the time was William M. Evarts, also a New Yorker, and interested in acquiring the obelisk. Consequently, no position was taken on the subject of slavery in Egypt for fear of antagonizing the Egyptian authorities. Moreover, the political climate in the United States, after the demise of Reconstruction in 1877 and the ascendancy of the South, was not conducive to the United States government taking a stand against slavery or the slave trade anywhere. The subject was strictly taboo, not to be raised by any prudent politician.

CONFLICTING SIGNALS FROM WASHINGTON

In his address on the occasion of presenting his letter of credentials, the New American Consul-General, Elbert E. Farman, praised the Khedive's government for its new institutions, internal improvements, and extended geographical explorations. He described Egypt as, "A country that numbers its years by thousands and possessing the oldest and greatest monuments of antiquity and at the same time showing an energy and love of progress that had given it a high rank in modern civilization.[1]

His remark was not only a normal diplomatic courtesy, but also the forerunner of a strong friendship which culminated in a major literary work defending the Khedive Ismail, and mercilessly attacking his adversaries, especially England and France.[2]

By this time the British official and public pressures to abolish slavery and the slave trade in the Nile Valley had turned into a bitter struggle between the British and Egyptian governments, with religious, political, economic and moral overtones. The British pressures were considered by the Khedive Ismail and his subjects as anti-Muslim and as undermining the political and economic sovereignty of Egypt. The appointment of Baker as governor of the Equatorial provinces, Gordon as his successor and then as Governor-General of the entire Sudan, the second most important job in the land, and the appointment by Gordon of fourteen Europeans in the top positions in his administration, further confirmed Egyptian fears.

The American community, especially those working in the Consulate, as well as the missionaries, were not happy with Farman's indifference to the question of slavery at a time when it was one of the major topics of discussion. Their concern was also the result of their interrelations with the various European communities whose memories of the American Civil War and the slavery era were still fresh.

After the opening of the Suez Canal, and even long before, Egypt had attracted many Europeans who clustered in several communities, competing for economic opportunities, comtemptuous of each other in a society which was hostile to them all. In such a climate, the American old-timers were not about to play a passive role toward the issue of slavery while their European counterparts were actively opposing it.

In March of 1876, Farman was taken by surprise by a memorandum from the State Department informing him that the Consulate-General's clerk, John Hay, had sent to them a report about the slave trade in the Nile Valley. A copy of the report was enclosed.[3] Farman found himself in a critical position. Since his arrival in May of the year before, he had not written one word on the subject of slavery, in spite of the fact that he was a prolific writer.

Thus, in response, Farman wrote a despatch in which he utilized his legal training. He bagan first by criticizing Hay for writing to the State Department over his head, since the consular instructions specified that all letters addressed to the Department should come through the Consul-General. Secondly, he attacked the authenticity of Hay's information in regard to the slave trade by saying that such information was based on rumors "derived form certain English journals hostile to Egyptian interests and whose paid correspondents regard it as more important, and find it much easier to produce readable and exciting articles than to ascertain and report fact.[4]

He concluded by saying that he had made inquiries into all the places he visited on his tours to inspect the consular agencies and that he intended to write "a true statement of the case and at the same time do not injustice to the government of the Khedive."[5]

Farman's reply, which was given in anger and defiance, would set the tone of his position toward the question of slavery in the Nile Valley. Unlike his predecessor, Richard Beardsley, he was not the idealist who was influenced by the humanitarian British anti-slavery movement. As a lawyer of almost twenty years experience, most of it during the Civil War and its aftermath, he was a different breed of man.

Apparently, the American community in Egypt decided to apply pressure to get the American Consulate involved in suppressing the slave trade. In June of 1877, an American citizen brought a slave boy of twelve to the Consulate to help him in obtaining his freedom papers. The boy was sent to the police with the Consulate Janissary (guard), and his papers were obtained without delay.

Farman sent a despatch to the State Department describing the incident, primarily to "show with what little difficulty slaves are freed." He continued by saying that any slave could procure his freedom by applying at a Consulate, upon which the Consul-General asked for the liberation of the slave, and the authorities immediately complied. Admitting that such applications are rare, Farman remarked that he had "acted in this case according to the usual custom. The boy will be sent to the American Mission School at Assiout and properly educated."[6]

When the Convention between Egypt and Britain for the Suppression of the Slave Trade was signed at Alexandria on August 4, 1877, Farman sent a copy of it to the State Department.[7] The Convention was spelled out in seven articles. Whenever the word 'slaves' appeared, it was followed by "negroes and Abyssinians." It prohibited the traffic in slaves and the mutilation of slave children immediately after the signing of the Convention in Egypt, and after three months in the rest of her dependencies. The rest of the articles specified punishments for the violators, and methods and means of implementing the Convention, including British and Egyptian cruisers' rights to search, and if necessary, detain vessels engaged or suspected of being engaged in the traffic in the Red Sea, in the Gulf of Aden, on the coast of Arabia, and in the maritime waters of Egypt and her dependencies. While Egyptian vessels in violation of the Convention were returned to the British authorities. The Egyptian government was to publish a special Ordinance prohibiting altogether traffic in slaves within Egyptian territories after a date to be specified in the Ordinance, and punishment of violaters.[8]

On the same day of the signing, the Khedive issued a decree providing that the private sale and purchase of slaves (negro and Abyssinian) should cease among families within seven years in Egypt proper (ending in 1884) and twelve years in the Sudan and other Egyptian dependencies (ending in 1889). Apart from this, the Khedival decree stipulated the prohibition of the traffic in slaves (blanc ou blanches) in Egypt and her dependencies within seven years of the date of the Convention.[9]

From the outset, the Convention and its annex were criticized. The Sultan resented the rights granted the British cruisers in Turkish territorial waters. The British Anti-Slavery Society was disappointed bacause it expected a more militant arrangement. Gordon, the Governor-General of the Sudan at the time, thought that the Khedive was forced to sign a treaty which he would not be able to implement. Farman's criticism stemmed from the fact that the Convention intentionally or not, ignored the existence of the "Caucasian and Georgian" slaves, and failed to "interfere in any manner with the peculiar oriental system of concubinage."[11] He made no reference to the Khedival decree prohibiting the slave trade in white women after seven years, the mention of which would have undermined the central point in his criticism. Nevertheless, his remarks exposed the hypocrisy of the co-signers of the Convention, especially the British, in omitting one kind of slavery in the text of a Convention whose purpose was to eradicate slavery.

In the meantime, the American society was witnessing the end of the period of Reconstruction and the withdrawal of the federal troops from the Southern states as a result of a compromise between the Republican and Democratic parties. After twelve years of political confrontation and bitterness over the question of slavery, and emancipated blacks and their rights, very few Americans were ready to deal with or inquire into the suppression of the slave trade in "negroes and Abyssinians" in the Nile Valley, or the continuing enslavement of white women. The New York Times headline, "The African Traffic in Egypt: No Sale For Africans and Abyssinians, But Trade in Circassians and Georgians Still Tolerated," was a direct outcome of Farman's calculated criticism. He succeeded in turning both the American establishment and the public against the Convention. Indeed Farman did not forsee any role for his government in the suppression of the slave trade in the Nile Valley.

Despite Farman's indifference, the American community in Cairo continued to bring slaves to the Consulate-General asking him to help them to obtain their freedom papers. In June of 1878, two American missionaries from Asyut brought three slave girls from Darfur. Farman related the story of their capture and journey as follows:

> Most of the journey was by river,
> but they were at one time a month
> on the desert. Ond of the slaves
> was disobedient and was shot.
> Another was beaten while on a
> camel and fell and died, either
> from the fall or from the effects
> of the blows, and a third who made
> complaints and some trouble on
> account of want of water while
> on the desert was tied to a tree
> and left. The other thirteen
> arrived a few days since at Asiout,
> two hundred and thirty miles

115

above Cairo. Here the three girls were separated from the rest of the party and sold for thirty napoleons, a little less than one hundred and sixteen dollars. The purchaser was about to bring them to Cairo to be resold when a liberated slave, also a native of Darfour, having learned the facts seized the girls as they were being taken through the streets at night on their way out of the city and took them to the house of Dr. Hogg.[12]

After describing the horrors of the "Middle Passage" of the slave trade in the Nile Valley, Farman devoted the rest of his despatch to the subject of slavery in Egypt. According to him, there were slaves in all the cities and large villages of Egypt in every native family that was able to have servants. But slavery in Egypt was "of the mildest form and wholly different from that formerly existing in the United States." He added that slaves used for farm labor could not be kept for profit since the expenditure for their upkeep was equal to wages paid the _fellah_ for farm labor. For that reason, "Slavery is here confined almost exclusively to the large towns and is principally connected with domestic life peculiar to the higher and middle classes of the Orient."[13]

As to the utility of slaves, Farman reported that they are mainly kept "for the convenience of the harem," and to given dignity and importance to the master rather than for service. He continued by saying that very few male slaves "either earn their living or desire to change their condition," so that although it was generally understood that they could obtain their freedom by applying to a European Consulate, "comparatively few of them avail themselves of this privilege." Farman added, "They certainly perform less labor and fare better, both as regards their manner of living and their personal treatment than the fellah."[14]

Farman's account of slavery in Egypt is both accurate and comprehensive. His purpose, it seems, was to say that slavery was not only mild in Egypt, but also a blessing compared to the lot of the _fellah_.

As far as material comfort was concerned, his argument was no doubt correct, but he deliverately and intelligently omitted the moral aspect of slavery--that it was against human nature and that it was wrong, no matter what the advantages accrued.

One cannot help but recall the contemporary argument, based on the sufferings and agonies that the black African went through during and after the Civil War, that a benevolent and paternalistic slave society had been good for slaves and their offspring. Whether Farman had used this argument himself or not is immaterial. What is important is that he, the product of another slave society, did not commit himself to a clear-cut denunciation of slavery on moral grounds in another society at a time when the emancipation of American blacks was causing divisiveness among the whites, and visiting unprecedented cruelty and brutality on the freed slaves and their offspring.

FARMAN ENVISIONS A U.S. ROLE

While spending his summer vacation in his hometown of Warsaw in New York state, Farman wrote a letter to F.W. Seward, the assistant Secretary of State, to discuss the subject of slavery in the Nile Valley, recounting the visit of the British Consul-General in Cairo who had asked him to bring the matter before his government. Farman admitted that "something could be done in this subject by the United States in the cause of humanity and without necessarily incurring much, if any, expenses or much responsibility."[15]

Four months later, in January of 1879, Evarts, the Secretary of State, responded to his despatch from New York, requesting Farman inquire whether the Khedive "would be willing to consider the subject of a treaty with the United States for the suppression of the slave trade, similar in its tenor to that with Great Britain." His instructions in this regard were as follows:

> In doing so you will of course bear
> in mind the considerations contained
> in your letter of September 25, 1878,
> respecting the extent of the coop-
> eration which this government might
> be expected, or able, to give, in

> furtherance of the laudable purpose
> in view. Your observations on
> that point are judicious, and meet
> with the approval of the Department.[16]

Farman was not able to approach the Egyptian government immediately because of internal political developments. But before submitting a formal communication concerning the desire of the United States government to sign a convention, he discussed the subject with the Sherif Pasha, Minister of Foreign Affairs, and made sure of his approval in advance. In his formal letter to Sherif Pasha, Farman assured him of the commitment to the task of the part of the United States government.

> Knowing as I do the sincere desire
> of the Government of His Highness
> the Khedive to ameliorate, as
> far as possible, the condition
> of the people placed under its
> guardianship and that one of the
> measures that would tend to the
> accomplishment of that result
> is the total extinction of the
> traffic in slaves and the preven-
> ting of this importation in its
> dominions and their exportation
> to those of the other states, I
> cannot doubt that it will be
> agreeable to it to have the moral,
> and, so far as it may be deemed
> practical, the material aid of
> the Government of the United States
> in the attainment of so desirable
> an object, and one as much in the
> interest of humanity as the sup-
> pression of the traffic in slaves
> throughout Egypt and all its
> provinces and dependencies.[17]

Four days later, the Minister of Foreign Affairs responded to Farman's letter. His response was short and to the point.

> In reply I hasten to inform you...
> that the Government of the Khedive,
> appreciating the generous purpose
> of the Government of the United

States, is ready to conclude such
a convention and place itself in
communication for that object with
such representative as the Cabinet
at Washington shall invest with
the necessary power and authority.[18]

In his accompanying despatch, Farman informed the
Secretary of State that it was advisable to use the
word 'convention' instead of 'treaty' because of the
peculiar relation existing between the governments of
the Khedive and that of the Sultan. He also noticed
that the Anglo-Egyptian Convention was originally
written in French and translated into English, which
translation was not accurate, according to him.

Farman submitted a draft version that was the same
in substance as the Anglo-Egyptian one for the Department's consideration. The principal change was
inserting the provisions of Annex A and the Ordinance
into the text of the convention to replace Article III
and the last clause of Article II, which would be
moved to replace Article V. Annex A had stipulated
the creation of a special bureau to "attend to all
that concerns slaves thus liberated." It also
specified that the Egyptians would provide for liberated
slaves, and find employment for the males and education
and training for the children. Annex A also included
the Khedival Decree which provided for the prohibition
of traffic in white slaves after seven years.[19]

It will be recalled that Farman had omitted the
inclusion of the Decree in his 1877 despatch in order
to serve his own purpose of undermining the British
Convention. His suggestion to move it to the text in
the United States' version was tentatively approved
by Sherif Pasha, who read the draft Farman had prepared.

The consent of the United States government to
sign a convention with Egypt, coupled with the eagerness
of the Egyptian government to do so, combined to
persuade Farman to change his tactics. His subsequent
despatches reflect this change.[20]

Farman had done most of the ground work for the
signing of the Convention, and the Egyptian government
was ready and eager to sign for reasons that had nothing
to do with slavery or the slave trade. At the time,
it was economically and politically beleaguered by

Great Britain and France, and badly needed a strong and neutral ally such as the United States.

In a personal letter to F.W. Seward, enclosed with the despatch and draft, Farman conveyed his wish to conclude the Convention before the first of July, "provided the Department desire it convenient to give the necessary instruction at a sufficiently early date.[21]

After the Khedive Ismail was deposed and succeeded by his son Tawfiq, Farman reported that the new Khedive had only one wife, and that he was "very unfavorable to the system of harem."[22]

As a result of the political changes in Egypt, a new cabinet was installed. The State Department instructed Farman to make "discreet inquiry in the proper quarter, to the end of ascertaining whether the new government will be dispensed to continue the negotiation begun with Sherif Pasha."[23]

Farman responded to the instruction from Warsaw, New York, with the information that Sherif Pasha still held the same ministerial positions as before, and that he knew of nothing which would indicate a change of policy in respect to the convention. He concluded that it would be "proper as well as politic to act on the presumption that the new government will follow the course as indicated in my despatch of May first.[24]

For nearly one year, nothing more was written about the convention or the slave trade. Then in May of 1880, Farman sent a despatch concerning the arrest of thirty-five slave merchants in Asyut with eighty-five slaves. The slaves were hidden in a mountain outside the town and the sale of slaves was conducted in secrecy. Farman reported:

> No secrecy would have been required
> except as to a few Europeans and
> converted Copts, and had it not
> been for the zeal of a young man
> by the name of Roth, a native of
> Switzerland and a teacher in the
> American Mission school at Assiout,
> the caravan would in the course
> of a few days have sold its slaves
> as well as other merchandize,

> bought its goods and necessary
> supplies, and disappeared among
> the mountains of the desert....

> Mr. Roth came the next day to
> Cairo to give information of what
> he had ascertained; and having
> learned that the English Government
> had a treaty with that of Egypt
> prohibiting the slave trade he
> went to the English Consul-General
> and stated to him the facts.[25]

Two weeks later, Farman sent another despatch in
which he praised the Egyptian government for its
immediate and firm action against the governor of Asyut
and his subordinates, who were collaborating with the
slave traders. He reported that Count Salla, the
Italian, was appointed Controller General for the
suppression of the slave trade. Farman was sympathetic
toward the Egyptian government in her efforts to
suppress the slave trade, and at times, even apologetic:

> It must nevertheless be admitted
> that however great the zeal or
> earnest the desire of the Khedive
> to end this nefarious system of
> stealing children from their
> homes in Central Africa and trans-
> porting them one or two thousand
> miles across the desert, subjecting
> them to privation and suffering
> which no pen can describe, and from
> which many of them die, His High-
> ness has difficulties to overcome
> that are almost insuperable and
> will remain so until slavery is
> actually abolished not only in
> Egypt, but throughout all the
> Ottoman Empire.[26]

In July of 1880, Farman was faced with a delicate
and embarrassing situation. Five slaves, owned by
Prince Hassan, the younger brother of the Khedive who
was exiled with his father, Ismail, came to the
Consulate-General seeking help in obtaining their
freedom papers. They said that while the Prince was
in Egypt they had been treated kindly, but after his
departure his <u>wakil</u> (superintendent) began treating

them with cruelty. Farman related the story of their capture as it was told to him by the slaves:

> On questioning them I found that
> they were born free in Central
> Africa south of Darfur; that about
> eight years ago an Egyptian general,
> whose name I refrain from mention-
> ing as he is still occupying a
> high position in Egypt, was
> carrying on a war in their country
> and subduing all the tribes in
> the region; that he burned the
> villages and killed and drove
> away many of the inhabitants; and
> that they with others were taken
> and made slaves. They served for
> some time in the army as porters
> and about four years ago were
> brought to Cairo and given to
> Prince Hassan. Two of them had
> marks upon thier faces....I asked
> them how they came to be marked
> in this manner and they all
> replied that when they were made
> slaves the General had them marked
> so that if they ran away they could
> be known....Whether taken and
> reduced to slavery they are marked
> as a herdman marks his animals.27

This account shows the discrepancy between the Egyptian officials' claims that slavery was illegal and the fact that it was still practiced by top officials, and even the royal family. Since the pressures for abolishing the slave trade were coming from outside, while the society itself condoned and practiced it, there evolved an understanding among the officials and the people of Egypt and Northern Sudan that slavery was a fact of life, as far as they were concerned; but as far as the outside would was concerned, slavery and the slave trade were abolished. The only solution for the slavery question in the Nile Valley was either through the development of internal opposition to the institution based on moral or religious reasons, or the introduction of an external power to take over the government and eradicate slavery and the slave trade by sheer force.

Farman sent the five slaves with a note in Arabic to the Bureau for the liberation of slaves, asking for their freedom "in accordance with the law and custom in such cases." He asked that the five be returned to the Consulate "otherwise it is always a question of doubt as to what is ultimately done with them." But his messenger returned after two or three hours without them. He was told that they were liberated and that "they must be put in the army; and as he learned they had been sent to prison, the common Arab jail."[28]

Farman decided to take up the matter with Riaz Pasha, Minister of Interior and President of the Council of Ministers. In Farman's opinion, to enter the army in Egypt meant going into perpetual servitude. When a young man was taken for a soldier in Egypt, he was considered as dead by the female members of his family. There was practically no pay for military service, and no slave, however badly treated, would be willing to change his conditions for that of an Egyptian soldier.

In spite of his intimate knowledge of slavery and the slave trade in the Nile Valley, and what had actually happened to the five slaves, Farman's approach to Riaz Pasha was circuitous:

> ...I stated to his Excellency that it appeared to me very unjust that these young men, who seemed to have more than ordinary capacity for persons of their class--having evidently been enlisted for the Prince on account of their brightness and fine physical condition-- should have been taken from their homes and brought two thousand miles to a strange country as slaves, and then, after being held for a number of years, should, on asking to be liberated, be given papers of manumission, it is true, but nevertheless be sent to jail in order to be afterwards transferred to the army. Much other conversation was had, which resulted in the Pasha giving an immediate written order for their liberation.[29]

The five men were finally freed, and expressed in their own "simple manner" their gratitude to Farman. One explanation for his lack of forcefulness in his approach could be that his government did not have a convention similar to that between Egypt and Great Britain. As a matter of fact, the United States government had apparently dropped the whole question of signing a convention, after the Egyptian government had given its approval. Although the absense of a convention made Farman's position weaker, the reasons for his easy, non-confrontational attitude lies elsewhere.

In October 1882 issue of Century Journal, Farman had written an article entitled, "The Negotiation for the Obelisk," in which he gave a detailed account of his activities between May of 1877 and the beginning of 1880, during which time he was busy making contacts with the Egyptian government trying to persuade them to give the city of New York an obelisk. The obelisk Farman had in mind was "Cleopatra's Needle," owned by the port of Alexandria. Such a gift would rob that city of the only obelisk then standing, and consequently constitute a major accomplishment for the United States in the field of Egyptology. Farman's negotiations initiated a fierce struggle between him and the British and French communities and their consular representatives in Cairo, and European archeologists who were in control of the Egyptian museums and antiquities at the time.

During the thirty months that Farman was engaged in these intrigues, he met with the Khedive Ismail and Khedive Tawfiq, and Presidents of the Council of Ministers Riaz Pasha and Sherif Pasha more than fifteen times—once every two months. The Secretary of State, William M. Evarts, and the Under Secretary, F.W. Seward, both from New York, were aware of Farman's efforts to obtain the obelisk for New York City. For this reason, Farman and his superiors were reluctant to antagonize the Egyptian government by making slavery an issue. Needless to add that neigher the United States government or the public were ready in the post-Reconstruction period to consider any treaty abolishing slavery so far away in the Nile Valley.

When Farman recommended the opening of a new consular agency in the port of Sawakin in the Sudan, his main reason was its commercial importance in

exporting hides, elephant tusks and other products of
Central Africa, part of which would be sent to the
United States. He nominated Demetrius Moscanos, a
Greek businessman, for the job.

During Farman's absence on annual leave, the
vice-consul, Comanos, another Greek, wrote a lengthy
despatch concerning slavery and the slave trade in the
Nile Valley. He referred to a letter from the consular
agent in Khartoum, Azar abd el Malak, an Egyptian
Copt, informing the Consulate-General of the arrest
of a number of merchants from Suakin with one hundred
and thirty slaves. Comanos mentioned that a Mr. Van
Dyke, the clerk of the Consulate-General helped one
slave and a eunuch in obtaining their freedom papers.
He also enclosed an article from the London Mail,
dated July 28, 1880. It contained several references
to the slave traffic as carried on between Africa and
Arabia across the Red Sea.

In the despatch Comanos supported Farman's
suggestion that a consular agency be opened at Suakin,
to aid in the suppression of the slave trade. He
also made a plea to the State Department to renew its
efforts to conclude the Slave Trade Suppression Convention with Egypt, and to join hands with Great
Britain "in the cause of freeing the enslaved."[30]

This despatch, despite its lack of organization
and eloquence that are characteristic of Farman's,
is clear and direct in its treatment of the subject
of slavery and the convention. Whereas Farman saw
the most important job that the consular agent in
Suakin would perform was commercial, Comanos looked
at it differently--to contribute on behalf of the
United States to the suppression of the slave trade.
He also expected to see the United States playing a
role similar in that respect to Great Britain.

Less than two months later the State Department
sent its reply, disapproving of the opening of a
consular agency in Suakin on the grounds that it did
not see any purpose that it would serve as far as
American interests were concerned.[31]

In April of 1881, Farman received a letter in
Arabic from the consular agent in Khartoum, Azar abd
El Malak, which contained detailed information about
the involvement of top Egyptian officials in the slave

125

trade, after the departure of Gordon Pasha, the former Governor-General. The letter, written by the Egyptian Copt who had lived for so many years in Khartoum, was the strongest condemnation yet of the Egyptian officialdom as far as the slave trade was concerned.

According to Azar, steep taxes had been imposed on the people of the Fashoda district. The Governor of Fashoda obtained the required sum by selling the children of the inhabitants into slavery, reporting the sales as being those of cattle, and forwarding the proceeds to the government. The Governor-General, Raouf Pasha, issued orders that the inhabitants must furnish young men for the army; thus forcing them to buy slaves to meet the army's demand. Azar added that the sale of slaves was going on throughout the Sudan, and that the Governor-General and governors owned slaves. He continued by reporting that Giegler Pasha himself went to Fashoda, discovered slaves in the households of the governor and some of his officers, and took the slaves to Khartoum. When the former Governor of Sennar was in charge of that district, said Azar, he seized and sold manumitted slaves to the inhabitants, who furnished them for the army. Also, merchants from the Hejjaz in Arabia, while in Khartoum, bought slaves and dispatched them to Arabia. The Governor of Berber intercepted them, and sent them to Khartoum. Furthermore, Arab cattle dealers in Kordofan regularly kidnapped children from the mountain regions and sold them as slaves, which practice went unnoticed by the district governors and the Governor-General. Azar concluded that "the rulers shut their eyes to the slave question, and their object is the continuation of the sale of slaves. This is what is now occurring.[32]

Farman used the information in this letter as justification for departing from his previous position of procrastination and indecision concerning slavery and slave trade in the Nile Valley. Finally he began to perceive a role for the United States in abolishing both institutions.

The same despatch, Farman enclosed a copy of an article written by an English judge in the London Times of May 19, 1881. The article referred to the continuous and brisk traffic in slaves on the Red Sea. It suggested that the total abolition of slavery was the true means and the most practical one of putting an end to the commerce in human beings.

126

Farman reversed his earlier position converning
the leniency with which the slaves from Sudan and
Central Africa were treated, saying:

> I do not agree with the writer in
> the article in the Times as to the
> fact of slaves in Egypt being
> rarely ill-treated. On the con-
> trary, I learn of many cases of
> the greatest barbarity. To say
> that they are as comfortable as
> the Egyptian peasant is no commen-
> dation of their conditions. The
> peasant, however as miserable they
> are, have their families. The
> slaves cannot marry the females
> being shut up during their whole
> lives as servants in the harems,
> rarely if ever seeing the outside
> of their prison walls, and never
> having any intercourse whatever
> with or even seeing the males
> perchance through the arabesque
> lattice work that cover their
> windows. Little is known concerning
> the treatment they receive at the
> hands of their Circassian mis-
> tresses, the latter being themselves
> slaves, but from the narrations
> of an occasional slave woman that
> escapes from her prisonkeepers,
> it is of that semi-barbarian
> character that one would naturally
> expect from the ignorant and
> cruel, though haughty race of the
> Caucasians,
>
> In any event this system of
> involuntary imprisonment is suf-
> ficiently bad to call for the
> moral condemnation of the civilized
> world.[33]

Farman continued to argue along those lines,
condemning slavery as being morally wrong and indefensible. Then he made the final departure from his
previous positions:

> If certain of the great powers
> would earnestly use their moral
> force to that purpose, it is very
> probable that in the present con-
> dition of Egypt, a decree might be
> obtained abolishing slavery. If
> this were done and the proper
> measures adopted relative to
> guarding the coasts of the Red Sea,
> slavery would not only be ended
> in Egypt but would in a short time
> substantially disappear throughout
> the entire Ottoman Empire.[34]

He further advocated that more radical measures
be adopted than those proposed, stating that the
treaty made between Egypt and Great Britain for the
suppression of the slave trade, although a step in
the right direction, had "proved wholly inadequate."[35]

In an unofficial letter to the Secretary of State,
James G. Blaine, Farman was even more forceful,
suggesting that the United States join with England
in an "earnest effort to bring about the abolition of
slavery in Egypt."[36] Questioning the interest of
other powers in the matter, as well as England's
sincerity in enacting the previous anti-slavery measures, Farman hypothesized:

> If however, the Britannic Majesty's
> Government should be interrogated
> relative to a joint effort of this
> kind, its real sincerity would be
> brought to the test, and if its
> object was the final abolition of
> slavery in the Orient, it would be
> likely to be willing to join the
> United States in measures designed
> to accomplish this object.

> There are good political reasons
> why our government would avoid all
> foreign complications, but I do
> not see the slightest danger or
> possibility of any complications
> arising out of the use of such
> moral force as we may possess to
> accomplish so desirable a result as
> the abolition of slavery in Egypt....

128

> Great credit would be due to a
> government which should take the
> initiative in the accomplishment
> of so laudable a work.

> I have made the suggestion contained
> in this letter only to call your
> attention to what may be an oppor-
> tunity to effect a result that will
> be commended not only by the present
> generation but by every succeeding
> one that shall be informed of the
> fact.[37]

Farman's claim that other European countries were
not interested in the matter was inaccurate. Two
months earlier a deputation of the British Anti-Slavery
Society proposed to the British government to establish
a mixed commission whose members would be French and
British to supervise the Slave Department in Egypt.
The deputation maintained that the French government
was sympathetic to British efforts in suppressing the
slave trade in the Nile Valley. Since both France
and England had been supervising the Egyptian finances
since 1876, the deputation argued that "if Europe
might supercede one of the primary rights of self-
government on behalf of her bond-holders, it was not
too much to say that she had a stronger right to
interfere on behalf of the claims of humanity."[38] By
the plan of a mixed commission, all of the offenders
of the slave trade decrees and conventions would be
dealt with under mixed tribunals, not under Egyptian
courts.[39]

It is interesting that Farman had suggested a role
for the American government only two months after the
suggestion of the British Anti-Slavery Society, which
was widely publicized in the London _Times_, March 19,
1881, and the _Anti-Slavery Reporter_, April 14, 1881,
without reference to such.[40]

One cannot help but ask what the causes were
behind Farman's change of position. To understand
them, one has to examine his motives. When Farman
accepted the relatively insignificant post of American
Consul-General in Egypt, he had already completed
twenty years of a lucrative law practice in New York.
From the start it was evident that he was over-qualified
for the job. His personal letters to Secretary of

State Evarts, also a New Yorker, showed that the two
men were close friends. Farman's eloquent defense
of Khedive Ismail in his book, and the State Department's dragging of its feet when it came to signing
a convention against slavery in Egypt were clearly
calculated to gain the friendship and support of the
Khedive in order to acquire the obelisk. When that
was successfully achieved, Farman, obtained as a
reward, a judgship in the Mixed Courts in Alexandria,
and resigned his post. Farman changed his stance in
regard to slavery only after the obelisk had left
Egypt.

He was succeeded by another consul-general,
Mr. Wolf, who arrived in Egypt in September of 1881.
In the same month, the Egyptian army under the leader-
ship of Arabi Pasha revolted. In the middle of August,
the Mahdia revolution broke out in the Sudan. Thus
the problem of slavery and the slave trade in the
Nile Valley became secondary as a result of the basic
political changes in Egypt and the Sudan.

Chapter VIII

THE MAHDIA AND THE UNITED STATES:
REACTIONS AND INTERPRETATIONS

The British occupation of Egypt in 1882 started
in earnest the European scramble for Africa. Under
the British, Egypt no longer served as the outlet
for slaves from the Sudan.

While the African continent was gradually
being divided among European powers, the Sudan,
under the banner of el Mahdi, was emerging as an
independent xenophobic state with no outside influence, until its final fall in 1898. Since the
eruption of the Mahdia in 1881, and especially after
the fall of Khartoum and the assassination of Gordon
in 1885, the Sudan was being ruled by an autocracy,
along the lines of Islam.

Although the discontent created by Gordon's
strict measures to suppress the slave trade in
the Sudan was among the main reasons behind the
outbreak of the Mahdia, and the slave merchants
were among its staunchest supporters, the Mahdia
was a religious and political revolution. Its
main object was to rid the Sudan of corrupt, oppres-
sive foreign rulers and to establish a state based
on the tenets of basic Islam. The Mahdi also en-
visioned himself as a man with a mission in the
Islamic world, and indeed, in the whole world.

As such, slavery and the slave trade were
not part of the ideology and practice of the Mahdia.
It was dealt with within the over-all tradition
of Islam. Slavery was tolerated, and those tribes
which were non-Muslim were considered as fair
game. This tradition fitted neatly into the patterns
of the historical development of the region. So
the slave trade continued, but without the main
outlets of Egypt and the Red Sea. It was confined
to the local markets, which were limited in scope
and capacity.

The Third Chapter dealt with the American
press coverage of the Mahdia, which was mainly derived from the British newspapers, whose hostile
attitude toward the Mahdia was understandable.

131

To them the Mahdi and his followers were a bunch of slave traders, an attitude that was shared by the British government and other Western powers.

CONSULAR DESPATCHES CONCERNING THE MAHDIA

The American Consulate-General in Cairo had paid little attention to the Mahdia until the beginning of 1884, when the question of Egyptian evacuation from the Sudan under British pressure became a serious issue in Anglo-Egyptian relations. A cable by cypher reached the State Department saying that as a result of British interference in the Sudan question, the Egyptian cabinet member resigned. [1] The cable was followed by a short despatch reporting that Sir Evelyn Baring, British Agent and Consul-General in Egypt, had asked the Egyptian government for complete evacuation and the establishing of a defense line at Wadi Halfa, near the Second Cataract.

George Pomeroy, who had succeeded Farman as Agent and Consul-General, added that the Egyptian cabinet could not agree to give up a huge region like the Sudan, where she had vital interests. It had no alternative but to resign under British pressure; and no government was formed. [2]

In a following despatch, Pomeroy reported that Riaz Pasha had declined to form a new government whose duty would be to evacuate the Sudan. Eventually, Nubar Pasha accepted to form a new government to execute the British policy of evacuation. [3]

Pomeroy criticized the British policy in Egypt, which he blamed for the suffering of Egypt and the loss of the Sudan. He advocated international intervention to guarantee Egyptian independence. In his opinion, such intervention would not weaken British influence because nine-tenths of the ships which crossed on the Suez Canal were British. He also attacked the British policy in the formation of an Egyptian army and her refusal to enlist Turkish mercenaries. The destruction of Hicks Pasha's expedition by the Mahdists in 1883 eventually led the British to change their minds and enlist Turkish and Nubian troops, but that step had come too late. Pomeroy quipped that Britain had succeeded in creating an army that was fit only for ceremonies and parades.

He continued by saying that most observers, native and foreign, agreed that the complete evacuation of the Sudan was an unwise decision. The subsequent events proved the validity of Sherif Pasha's opinion, that the evacuation of the Sudan would cost Egypt more than maintaining a government in the Sudan. The Mahdist revolution had grown so strong and the number of its followers increased to such an extent that it began to create fears and doubts. If no precautions were taken, the Mahdists would soon be marching into Egypt proper.

Pomeroy criticized the belief that Gordon would succeed single-handedly in effecting the evacuation. He accused the British of contradicting themselves by sending Gordon as peace emissary to the Sudan, while despatching troops to fight Osman Digna, a Mahdist commander in Eastern Sudan. He asked what the Sudanese would think of the British emissary of peace, the white Madhi, while his compatriots were shooting them. [4]

The lengthy despatch contained a careful analysis of the political situation in Egypt and Sudan at that time. Although he referred to the Mahdia several times, he did not mention the slave trade as one of its objectives. This despatch differs widely in this respect from the American newspapers' coverage.

On July 17, 1884, Pomeroy received a cable from Washington informing him that the consulate-general was cancelled by Congress, and that his salary was stopped as of the fifth of the month. He was instructed to close the consulate-general immediately, and to leave Cairo at his convenience. [5] The Congress had passed the resolution in spite of the efforts of the State Department to save the consulate-general. When the vice-consul, Comanos, volunteered to run the consulate-general without pay, the State Department accepted readily. Funds were provided for basic expenses only.

The period between the end of 1884 and the beginning of 1886 was one of silence as far as the Sudan and the Mahdia were concerned. It was during this period that the Mahdia was able to establish its hegemony over the whole of Sudan, except for the port of Suakin and a few stations in Equatoria, where the Egyptian troops were trapped. The areas that were the traditional sources of slaves were overrun, and the population was voluntarily or by force converted to Islam under the banner of the Mahdia. Those who were captured during or after the confrontation were turned into slaves and became property of the state, which conscripted them into the army.

After the re-opening of the Consulate-General in October of 1885, there was no reference to the slave trade in the despatches sent by the consular-general, necessitating the State Department to inquire whether the slave trade was still in existence in Egypt. The response of the Consul-General was very short, claiming that there was no "systematic slave trade in Egypt."[6]

It is not quite clear why the State Department inquired about the slave trade in Egypt at that time. Furthermore, it is not clear what the Consul-General meant by "systematic trade." He confirmed, however, that an unsystematic slave trade was still going on; but he did not elaborate.

Between 1877 and 1889, the Manumission Bureaus in Egypt had manumitted twenty-thousand slaves. After the Brussels Conference in 1889, one of whose aims was to put "an end to the crimes and devastation engendered by the traffic in African slaves," the Egyptian government intensified its anti-slavery policy. This policy, which included a "general act for the repression of the African slave trade," published July 2, 1890, was so successful that at the end of 1893, some Egyptian ministers proposed to abolish the Slave Trade Department on the grounds that slavery was extinct. The British, however, refused to abandon this Department, as they were sure that without it the trade would revive. [7]

The far-sightedness of the British was rewarded when in August of 1894, three top officials in the Egyptian government were arrested by the British authorities in Cairo, accused of purchasing six Sudanese female slaves. In reporting the incident, the American Vice-Consul Mitchell said:

> In view of the fact that the Government
> of the United States is party to the
> treaty for the suppression of the
> slave trade to which Egypt gave its
> adherence in the year 1877, thereby
> abolishing slavery in its territories,

134

> I have thought it proper to inform
> the Department of the arrests now
> transpiring. I therefore transmit
> herewith an extract from the
> Egyptian Gazette of yesterday's
> date, the statements in which I
> have substantially verified. [8]

The three Pashas and others were court-martialled. The first two were acquitted, but the British commander-in-chief of the Egyptian army refused to approve the acquittal, and asked for a retrial. A serious crisis ensued; a compromise was reached. Sherif Pasha, Speaker of the Legislative Assembly, and one of the accused, would admit his guilt in writing, and he would be pardoned on the grounds of poor health.

The case against those prominent Egyptian dignitaries was meant by the British to bring the slave trade and slavery in Egypt to a definite end. The humiliation and threat of imprisonment to those leaders meant that no one was too big for the law, when it came to slavery - an awesome reminder to the rest of Egypt that slavery was no longer tolerated or accepted. The case also brought to light that the slave trade had been continuing to flourish in the Sudan, and that a few of the slaves had found their way into Egypt, where there had still been a demand for them in the middle class and aristocracy.

The comment of the American vice-consul is puzzling. His was, no doubt, the first interpretation of its kind in the documents of United States involvement in the question of slavery in the Nile Valley. To say that the United States was indirectly a party to the Anglo-Egyptian Convention because of its participation in an earlier agreement is interesting. It is not clear to which agreement he was referring. It could have been one of the early agreements concerning the Trans-Atlantic slave trade, or something more recent as the one Leopold II of Belgium had called for in 1876, from which developed the International African Association, or the agreement which arose from the Brussels Conference of 1889. Whatever the case might have been, the vice-consul's intriguing interpretation was not shared by either the previous American consuls-general in Egypt, or by the State Department officials in Washington.

The final act against slavery came on November 21, 1895, at which time a new convention, more comprehensive than that of 1877, was signed between Great Britain and Egypt. [9] Its double aim was to abolish slavery completely, and to help those slaves already liberated, any infringements against whom were classified as a severe crime. In 1896, two decrees were issued by the Egyptian government for the execution of this Convention, setting down the penalties for breaking it, and the procedure for abolishing slavery. The penalty for importing slaves to Egypt was up to fifteen years of hard labor. The decree also secured the surveillance of the Red Sea ports to prevent slave trading. [10]

BRITISH OCCUPATION OF THE SUDAN

United States interest in the Sudan was revived in 1896, when the British began organizing the campaign for the reconquest and occupation of the Sudan. In a long despatch describing the preparation for the final confrontation at Karrari, it was reported that among the top advisors of Kitchener, the British commander-in-chief of the campaign, was the Sudanese Zubair Rahama Pasha, depicted as the famous slave trader. It was also reported in the same despatch that one of Zubair's sons, who had been a prisoner of the Khalifa for years, had fled and joined the invading army, and had supplied the intelligence branch of the campaign with valuable information that helped in planning its strategy. [11]

On September 4, 1898, the consulate-general cabled the State Department concerning the fall of Omdurman and the defeat of the Khalifa and his army. [12]

On January 20, 1899, a copy of the Anglo-Egyptian Agreement for the Administration of the Sudan was sent to the State Department. Article XI read, "The importation of slaves in the Sudan, as also their exportation, is absolutely prohibited. Provision shall be made by the Proclamation for the enforcement of this regulation." Lord Cromer, who signed by Great Britain, wrote about the Sudan at the time, "Political issues are few in number and relatively simple in character. The most important, probably, is how slavery may be completely abolished without causing serious disorder." [13]

Except for a few incidents, particularly on the Ethiopian-Sudanese borders, slavery and the slave trade in the Sudan were coming to an end. In June of 1901, the American Consul in Cairo wrote that the fall of the Khalifa and the establishment of the Anglo-Egyptian administration had led to the eradication of the slave trade in the Sudan except on the Ethiopian-Sudanese borders and Nuba Mountains. The despatch reported that the end of slavery as an institution in the Sudan would be difficult to achieve, because in order to achieve such an end, many complicated problems would have to be solved first. [14]

Interestingly enough, this despatch led to the American protest to the Italian government, which denied any existence of the slave trade along the Sudanese-Eritrean borders. When the Italian response was conveyed to the American Consul-General in Cairo, he insisted on his accusation, and promised to provide the State Department with concrete evidence of the existence of slave trading activities along the Sudanese-Eritrean borders. [15]

The American protest to the Italian government, at a time when slavery and the slave trade were dying in the Nile Valley for the first time in its long history was certainly a valiant and chivalrous gesture, a gesture whose noble intentions should not be tarnished in any way because of its occurrence at the very, very last moment.

CONCLUSION

American reactions and conceptions of slavery and the slave trade in the nineteenth-century Nile Valley were varied, complicated, and constantly changing. They stand in stark contrast to the British official and humanitarian actions and reactions; but compare favorably with the apathy, vacillation, and covert and overt resistance of the government and populace of the Nile Valley.

The fact that the Nile Valley was considered by the American policy makers to be part of the "Eastern Question," which was in turn assumed to be part of the problems of the Old World, precluded any serious United States involvement in the thorny question of the abolition of slavery and the slave trade. Furthermore, the absence of politican and strategic interests, or significant commercial relations between the two regions, or a sizable resident American community in the Nile Valley gave the successive United States administration freedom from the pressure of having to take any moral position on the issue. This freedom from pressure was sustained by the continued silence of American religious groups, and by the fact that the anti-slavery societies were dissolved after the Civil War.

The several suggestions and appeals of Consuls-General Beardsley and Farman were either toyed with for a short while and then abandoned by bureaucrats in Washington, or ignored for fear of running the risk of antagonizing the intransigent and uncompromising Southern constituency to which the subject of the abolition of slavery and the slave trade was anathema. Morality was conveniently used when it served a purpose, e.g., in forcing France and Egypt to stop the further despatch of black Sudanese troops to Mexico and to withdraw those already there. Otherwise political expediency prevailed in Washington.

Paradoxically, the Civil War had a positive and a negative impact on the course of abolition in the Nile Valley. The cotton boom, brought on by the rise of Egyptian cotton exports as a result of the Union's embargo on southern ports, led to a tremendous increase in the ability of the upper and middle classes to purchase slaves. The suppliers in Khartoum and Constantinople were happy to meet the rising demand.

This negative effect, however, was more than offset by the efforts of the American officers, both Northerners and Southerners, in the Egyptian army who contributed to its modernization and effectivenss. Their surveying and mapping in the Sudan aided Baker and Gordon in their efforts to combat the slave traders. The officers also helped in military and administrative capacities. Judge Pierre Crabites claimed rather boastfully in his book, <u>Americans in the Egyptian Army</u>, that his compatriots had inculcated in the minds of young Egyptian officers the spirit of democracy and individualism which had eventually led to 'Arabi's revolt. Unfortunately, the abolition of slavery and the slave trade was not among the priorities of 'Arabi and his colleagues.

The American missionaries' reaction was similar to that of the United States government, in that they chose expediency over taking a moral stance. But theirs was more justifiable than that of their government. Operating in a predominantly Muslim country that looked upon their activities with hostility and suspicion, they had no alternative but to deal with the issue gingerly. Egyptian converts, mainly recruited from among the Copts, were discouraged from owning slaves, which represented a significant risk of losing such converts in a country where both Muslim and Coptic authorities conveniently ignored the practice. It is to the credit of the missionaries that they opened their schools to freed slaves. Their main contribution was in the field of education, where they helped in accelerating the pace of modernization and Westernization, and in creating an enlightened, tolerant social and political atmosphere that made the acceptance of the abolition of slavery and the slave trade in Egypt less disruptive and humiliating to a region with a glorious past and a universal religion.

It is important, however, to mention in this respect that the presence of the American officers and missionaries in the Nile Valley also added to the already deep fears, hostility, and paranoia of the Muslim population, and made them less receptive to Western pressures and values.

As far as the British government and populace were concerned, the moralistic position was affordable. The American official and unofficial positions, along with those of its counterparts in the Nile Valley, were predictable. Evidently more research is needed to explore the question of why the United States produced an indigenous abolition movement, which culminated in a protracted civil war and the final abolition of slavery, while the Nile Valley failed to produce such a movement, and required foreign intervention and domination in order to bring slavery and the slave trade to an end. Cultural, religious, and economic factors were involved in the way these two slave societies responded to abolition and its aftermath.

The American reactions to and conceptions of slavery and the slave trade in the Nile Valley can only be fully understood within this yet unexplored area of comparative slavery. The exchange between Prince Halim and the American Consul-General is revealing in this respect.* In it the representatives of two slave societies and governments exchange accusations and justifications which they knew very well were not true. Theirs was more than self-deception; it was an indirect admission that slavery in any way or form was against human nature, and therefore was indefensible.

*   See Appendix A

APPENDICES

APPENDIX A

Letter to the United States Secretary of State,
William H. Seward from the United States Consul-
General in Egypt, William S. Thayer, Alexandria,
March 25, 1863

Dear Sir:

Having nothing important in the way of public
information, I have concluded to write you a private
letter . . . .

On Sunday last I received as a present fresh
from the Soudan (Central Africa) a slave girl ten
years of age - an exceedingly handsome little black
[child]. Oriental consulates enjoy the privilege
of extraterritoriality. The girl was of course free
by the act of her master . . . within the exclusive
jurisdiction of the U.S., I suppose, and she hardly
required the benefit of Proclamation. However, I
told her she was free and put her in the hands of
my friend Lady Duff Gordon who will take her to England
and give her every proper advantage of good treatment
and education. The slave trade, though forbidden,
is secretly carried on in Egypt, and I am told that
this little black would bring, if sold, at least one
hundred dollars. By the way, I have been notified
of my election as a member of a Paris Anti-Slavery
Society of which I never heard until the arrival of
the circular informing me of my election. The Society
claims Daniel Webster among the list of its members,
and many European celebrities. I have not accepted.
Is it safe to follow Webster on the slavery question?

Last Sunday I visited Halim Pacha the young
uncle of the Vice Roy, and second in the order of
succession to the Vice Royalty, which does not descent
in the direct line, but to the oldest male of Mehemet
Ali's family . . .

Halim Pacha, though a Turk, and indulging in
the oriental luxury of a populous harem, etc., was
educated in Paris, and has the manners and accomplish-
ments of a European gentleman . . . .

143

He then asked me the news from America. Our war, he thought, would not be ended with the taking of Richmond or Vicksburgh; the Southern armies and generals had shown excellent strategy but our armies had improved greatly under the discipline of war . . . .

Incidentally he remarked that the Americans appeared to be the most aristocratic of people in spite of their republican institutions, as was shown by their prejudice against free blacks, a prejudice existing nowhere else. In Egypt black slaves may marry in the family of their owners and become free. His Highness cited an instance where a woman, formerly a slave, but with a trifle of black blood in her veins, having taken passage on a steamer from Liverpool to the U.S., almost caused an insurrection among the Americans aboard the ship who refused to sit at the common table with her. Afterwards he believed the woman prosecuted the Captain and got damages for her exclusion.

In reply, I said, that the American prejudice against free blacks was greatly exaggerated by foreign writers, that it was diminishing, and that it prevailed in the strongest degree among the least enlightened classes, especially among the more ignorant European emigrants. But in fact, in several states, political equality was already enjoyed by the blacks and perhaps the gradual progress of events (for such changes always require time) social equality might follow . . . But the prejudice against blacks among us did not, in my opinion, arise as much from antipathy to their color as from the fact that that color was a badge of a very numerous degraded class, and contempt of a degraded class was a failing not confined to any particular country. Even in Egypt we see it in the maltreatment of the Arab fellah by the ruling race. "Yes," exclaimed Halim Pacha, "but ours is a despotic, yours, a republican government." I admitted that his was a pertinent answer, but suggested that nevertheless the universal existence of his contempt of inferiors showed that the weakness of human nature would crop out under every system of government.

I write this to give you an idea of the way of thinking of an enlightened Turkish Prince and I hope you will not deem the report superfluous or too long . . .

APPENDIX B

Convention between Egypt and Great Britain for the
Suppression of the Slave Trade, signed at
Alexandria, 4 August 1877

The Government of Her Majesty the Queen of the
United Kingdom of Great Britain and Ireland, and the
Government of His Highness the Khedive of Egypt, being
mutually animated by a sincere desire to co-operate
for the extinction of the Traffic in Slaves, and having
resolved to conclude a Convention for the purpose
of attaining this object, the Undersigned, duly
authorized for this purpose, have agreed upon the
following Articles: --

ART. I.   The Government of His Highness the
Khedive having already promulgated a law forbidding
the Trade in Slaves (negroes or Abyssinians) within
the countries under His Highness' authority; engages
to prohibit absolutely from henceforward the importation of any slaves (negroes or Abyssinians) into any
part of the territory of Egypt or her dependencies,
or their transit through her territories, whether
by land or sea; and to punish severely, in the manner
provided by existing Egyptian law, or in such manner
as may hereafter be determined, any person who may
be found engaged, directly or indirectly, in the Traffic
of Slaves (negroes or Abyssinians).   The Government
of His Highness the Khedive further engages to prohibit absolutely any negroes or Abyssinians from leav-
ing the territory of Egypt or her dependencies, unless
it be proved indubitably that such negroes or
Abyssinians are free or manumitted.

It shall be stated in the certificates of
manumission or passports which shall be delivered
to them by the Egyptian authorities before their
departure that they may dispose of themselves without
restriction or reserve.

II.   Any person who, either in Egypt or on the
confines of Egypt and her dependencies toward the
centre of Africa, may be found engaged in the Traffic
in Slaves (negroes or Abyssinians), either directly
or indirectly, shall, together with his accomplices,
be considered by the Government of the Khedive
as guilty of "stealing with murder" ("vol avec
meurtre"): if subject to Egyptian jurisdiction he

145

shall be handed over for trial to a court-martial;
if not he shall immediately behanded over for trial
according to the laws of his country to the competent
tribunals, with the depositions ("proces-verbaux")
drawn up by the Egyptian superior authority of the
place where the traffic has been proved, and all other
documents or evidence ("elements de conviction")
handed over by the said authority, and destined to
serve as proofs at the trial of the traders, so far
as those laws may admit of such proof.

All slaves (negroes or Abyssinians) found in
the possession of a dealer in slaves shall be liberated
and dealt with in conformity with the provisions of
Article III and of Annex (A) to the present Convention.

III.   Taking into consideration the impossibility
of sending back to their homes slaves (negroes or
Abyssinians) who may be captured from slave-dealers and
liberated, without exposing them to the risk of perish-
ing from fatigue or want, or of falling again into
slavery, the Egyptian Government will continue to
take and apply in their favour such measures as they
have already adopted, and which are hereinafter
enumerated in Annex (A) to the present Convention.

IV.   The Egyptian Government will exert all the
influence it may possess among the tribes of Central
Africa, with the view of preventing wars which are
carried on for the purpose of procuring the selling
slaves.

It engages to pursue as murderers all persons who
may be found engaged in the mutilation of or traffic
in children: if such persons are amenable to Egyptian
jurisdiction they will be brought before a court-
martial; if not they will be handed over to the competent tribunals to be dealt with according to the law
of their country directs, together with the depositions ("proces-verbaux") and other documents or evidence ("elements de conviction") as laid down in
Article II.

V.   The Egyptian Government engages to publish
a special Ordinance, the text of which shall be annexed
to be present Convention, prohibiting altogether all
Traffic in Slaves within Egyptian territories after
a date to be specified in the Ordinance, and providing
also for the punishment of persons guilty of violating
the provisions of the Ordinance.

VI. With the view to the more effectual suppression of the Traffic in Slaves (negroes or Abyssinians) in the Red Sea, the Egyptian Government agrees that British cruizers may visit, search, and, if necessary, detain, in order to hand over to the nearest or most convenient Egyptian authority for trial, any Egyptian vessel which may be found engaged in the Traffic in Slaves (negroes or Abyssinians), as well as any Egyptian vessel which may fairly be suspected of being intended for that Traffic, or which may have been engaged in it on the voyage during which she has been met with.

This right of visit and detention may be exercised in the Red Sea, in the Gulf of Aden, on the coast of Arabia, and on the East Coast of Africa, and in the maritime waters of Egypt and her dependencies.

All slaves (negroes or Abyssinians) captured by a British cruizer on board an Egyptian vessel shall be at the disposal of the British Government, who undertakes to adopt efficient measures for securing to them their freedom.

The vessel and her cargo, as well as the crew, shall be handed over for trial to the nearest or most convenient Egyptian authority.

Nevertheless, in all cases where it may not be possible for the commander of the cruizer making the capture to forward the captured slaves to a British depot, or where from any other circumstances it may appear desirable and in the interest of the captured slaves (negroes or Abyssinians) that they should be handed over to the Egyptian authorities, the Egyptian Government engages on an application being made to them by the commander of the British cruizer, or by an officer deputed by him for that purpose, to take over charge of the captured negroes or Abyssinians, and to secure to them their freedom, with all the other privileges stipulated for or on behalf of negroes or Abyssinians captured by the Egyptian authorities.

The British Government, on its part, agrees that all vessels navigating under the British flag in the Red Sea, in the Gulf of Aden, along the coast of Arabia and the East Coast of Africa, or in the inland waters of Egypt and her dependencies, wich may be found engaged in the Traffic in Slaves (negroes or Abyssinians), may be visited, seized, and detained by the Egyptian authorities; but it is agreed that the vessel and its cargo shall, together with its crew, be handed over to the nearest British authority for trial.

The captured slaves (negroes or Abyssinians) shall be released by the Egyptian Government, and shall remain at their disposal.

If the competent tribunal should decide that the seizure, detention, or prosecution was unfounded, the Government of the cruizer will be liable to pay to the Government of the prize a compensation appropriate to the circumstances of the case.

VII.   The present Convention shall come into operation from the date of the signature hereof for Egypt proper as far as Assouan, and within three months from the date of signature for the Egyptian possessions in Upper Africa and on the shores of the Red Sea.

In witness whereof the Undersigned have signed the present Convention, and have affixed thereto their seals.

Done at Alexandria, this 4th day of August, 1877.

(L.S.)   C. VIVIAN.   (L.S.)   C. VIVIAN.
(L.S.)   CHERIF.   (L.S.)   CHERIF.

Convention Between Great Britain
and Egypt for the Suppression of
Slavery and the Slave Trade.

Signed at Cairo, November 21, 1895.

Whereas the general terms of the Convention of
the 4th August, 1877, between the British and
Egyptian Governments for the suppression of the Slave
Trade, as also the Decrees connected with it, have
left the point open to doubt whether the purchasers
of slaves were punishable as co-responsible with,
or accomplices of, the slave-merchants, whose traffic
they provoke and allow;

Whereas there is ground for adopting every means
of attaining the abolition of slavery;

Whereas the moment has come when the jurisdiction
in the matter of crimes and offences connected with
slavery, which is now exercised by courts-martial,
may be granted to Judges of the Native Courts;

Whereas it is of importance to combine the several
provisions relative to slavery;

The Government of Her Majesty the Queen of the
United Kingdom of Great Britain and Ireland, on the
one part, and the Government of His Highness the
Khedive of Egypt, on the other part;

Having resolved to remodel the said Convention
of the 4th August, 1877, by introducing into it the
modifications and additions that are required;

The Undersigned, duly authorized for this purpose,

Have agreed to substitute for the former Convention of the 4th August, 1877, the Convention which
follows hereafter: --

ARTICLE I.

The Government of His Highness the Khedive
undertakes to prohibit absolutely the importation
into any part of the territory of Egypt, and of its
dependencies, and the transit by land or by sea, across

such territory, of white, negro, or Abyssinian slaves destined for sale.

It undertakes also to prohibit absolutely the export from the territory of Egypt, or of its dependencies, of such persons, unless it be established for certain that they are free or emancipated.

It shall be recorded, in the letters of enfranchisement, or in the passports which shall be delivered to them by the Egyptian authorities before their departure, that they are free to dispose of their persons without restriction or reserve.

The traffic in such slaves is, and shall remain, prohibited throughout the whole extent of the territory of Egypt and its dependencies.

ARTICLES II.

The Egyptian Government undertakes to publish a Law setting forth the various breaches of the Conventions and Decrees relating to the suppression of the Slave Trade and the abolition of slavery, and, in general, all crimes and offences relative thereto, and the penalties attached.

In this Law it shall be stipulated that the purchasers of slaves shall be punished.

The said Law shall be published within six months from the signature of the present Convention, of which it shall form an integral part.

ARTICLE III.

Infractions of the Law which is provided for in Article II shall, when the accused is amenable to Egyptian jurisdiction, be referred to a Court of ultimate appeal, consisting of five Councillors of the native Court of Appeal, two of whom, at least, shall be Europeans.

Crimes and offences committed in the ports or on the shores of the Red Sea, and in the maritime zone defined in Article VII following, as well as in the territory subject to Egypt to the south of Assouan, shall continue to be judged by courts-martial.

The Egyptian Government undertakes to publish within six months from the date of the signature of the present Convention a Decree defining the procedure to be adopted by the Special Court and the court-martial in respect of the trial and passing of sentences.

ARTICLE IV.

If the accused be not amenable to Egyptian jurisdiction, he shall be immediately handed over for trial to the competent Tribunals, together with the depositions drawn up by the superior Egyptian authority of the place where the breach of the law shall have been established, and with all other documents or incriminating evidence.

ARTICLE V.

Every slave on Egyptian territory is entitled to his full and complete freedom, and may demand letters of enfranchisement whenever he desires to do so.

ARTICLE VI.

The Egyptian Government shall use all the influence which it may possess among the tribes of Central Africa with a view to prevent the wars which they are in the habit of making upon one another in order to procure and to sell slaves.

ARTICLE VII.

With a view to the more effective suppression of the Slave Trade, the Egyptian Government agrees that British cruisers may visit, search, and, if need be, detain, any Egyptian vessel under 500 tons which shall be found engaged in the Slave Trade, as well as any Egyptian vessel of the same tonage which shall be justly suspected of being intended for that trade, or which shall have taken part in it during the voyage on which it shall have been met.

It shall be lawful to exercise this right of visit or of detention within a zone extending between, on the one hand, the shores of the Indian Ocean (including those of the Persian Gulf and of the Red Sea), from Beluchistan to the point of Tangalane (Quilimane), and on the other hand, a conventional line which at

151

first shall follow the meridian of Tangalane as far as the point where it meets the 26th degree of south latitude, then becomes one with this parallel, then passes eastwards round the island of Madagascar, keeping at a distance of 20 miles from the eastern and northern coast till it cuts the meridian of Cape Amber. From this point the boundary of the zone shall be determined by an oblique line passing at a distance of 20 miles from Cape Ras-el-Had, and rejoining the coast of Beluchistan.

All slaves captured by a British cruiser on board an Egyptian vessel shall remain at the disposal of the British Government, which agrees to take effective measures for insuring their freedom.

The vessel and cargo, as well as the crew, shall be handed over to such Egyptian authorities as shall be nearest or most suitable in order that they may be tried by the court-martial referred to in Article III.

Nevertheless, in those cases where the Commanding Officer of the cruiser which has effected the capture shall find himself unable to consign the captured slaves to a British depot, or when it shall otherwise appear advisable, and in the interest of the captured slaves, that they should be handed over to the Egyptian authorities, the Egyptian Government undertakes, on receiving a request to that effect, either from the Commanding Officer of the British cruiser, or the officer delegated by him for that purpose, to take charge of the captured slaves, and assure them their freedom with all other privileges reserved for slaves captured by the Egyptian authorities.

The British Government on its part agrees to allow every vessel flying the British flag within the maritime zone above defined, which shall be found engaged in Slave Trade, to be visited, seized, or detained by the Egyptian authorities, but it is understood that the vessel and its cargo, as well as the crew, shall be handed over for trial to the nearest British authority.

The captured slaves shall be set free by the Egyptian Government, and shall remain at its disposal.

If the competent Tribunal decide that the seizure, detention, or prosecution, is not justified, the Government to which the cruiser belongs shall be liable to pay to the Government to which the other vessel belongs an indemnity appropriate to the circumstances.

ARTICLE VIII.

The present Convention shall come into operation from the date on which the Law respecting the crimes and offences connected with the Slave Trade, and the Law regulating the procedure to be adopted by the Courts authorized to deal with them--which Laws the Government of Egypt has hereinbefore undertaken to publish within six months from the signature of the present Convention--shall have acquired binding force.

The Convention of the 4th August, 1877, and the Decrees connected with it, shall cease to have effect from the day on which this Convention comes into operation, but in the meanwhile the Convention of the 4th August, 1877, and the Decrees connected with it, shall remain operative.

In witness whereof the Undersigned have signed the present Convention, and have affixed thereto their seals.

Done at Cairo, this 21st day of November, 1895.

(L.S.   CROMIER,
     Minister Plenipotentiary,
      Her Britannic Majesty's
      Agent and Consul-General
      in Egypt.

Annex (A).

Forming an integral part of the
Convention signed between the
British and Egyptian Governments,
on the 21st November, 1895.

The Government shall continue, as heretofore,
to maintain a special Department for the suppression
of the Slave Trade.

This Department shall be charged with all business
in connection with slaves and their enfranchisement.
It will retain control over the manumission offices
which are established in each Province or Governmental
district. These offices shall provide for everything
connected with slaves and their enfranchisement.

New manumission offices may be established if
necessary.

The Department for the suppression of the Slave
Trade shall have at its disposal a special force to
keep watch over the roads leading from the Desert
as well as the shores of the Red Sea, and generally
all places through which slaves enter Egyptian territory
either for importation or transit.

The Department for the suppression of the Slave
Trade is charged with the duty of insuring the strict
application of the Laws and Regulations affecting
the Slave Trade and slavery; of tracing guilty persons
and bringing them before the proper Courts, with proofs
in support of the charge.

CROMER.

Consular Officers by Post: Egypt, 1835-1899

Egyptian Rulers	American Consular Agents and Consuls	Place	Date
Mohammed Ali 1805-1849	Gliddon, John	Alex.	1835
	Gliddon, George R.	Cairo	1836
	Todd, Alexander	Alex.	1844
	Humphrey, Henry B.	Alex.	1846
	Consuls-General		
Abbas 1849-1854	Macauley, Daniel S.	Alex.	1848
	Jones, Richard B.	Alex.	1852
	De Leon, Edwin	Alex.	1853
Said 1854-1863	Thayer, William S.	Alex.	1861
	Hale, Charles	Alex.	1864
	Taylor, George C.	Cairo	1864
Ismail 1863-1879	Butler, George H.	Alex.	1870
	Beardsley, Richard	Alex.	1872
	Barthow, Victor	Cairo	1871
	Diplomatic Agents and Consuls-General		
Tewfik 1879-1892	Farman, Elbert E.	Cairo	1876
	Wolf, Simon	Cairo	1881
	Pomeroy, George	Cairo	1882
	Cardwell, John	Cairo	1886
	Schuyler, Eugene	Cairo	1889
	Anderson, John	Cairo	1891
Abbas Helmi 1892-1914	Little, Edward C.	Cairo	1892
	Penfield, Frederic	Cairo	1893
	Harrison, Thomas S.	Cairo	1897
	Long, John C.	Cairo	1899

NOTES

INTRODUCTION: SLAVERY AND THE SLAVE TRADE IN THE NILE
VALLEY

1   Bernard Lewis, Race and Color in Islam (New York:
     Harper and Row, 1971), p. 81.

2   Ahmed E. ElBashir, "Azar Abdel Malak, The Second
     U.S. Consular Agent in Khartoum," in Arabic,
     Bulletin of Sudanese Studies, VII (February,
     1981), 7.

3   Broge Fredriksen, Slavery and its Abolition in
     Nineteenth-Century Egypt, Ph.D. dissertation,
     University of Bergen, Sweden, 1977, p. 96.

4   Abbas I. M. Ali, The British, the Slave Trade and
     Slavery in the Sudan, 1820-1881 (Khartoum:
     University of Khartoum Press, 1972), p. 96.

5   Fredriksen, op. cit., p. 177.

6   Encyclopedia of Islam, Vol. I, 37.

7   Fredriksen, op. cit., p. 145.

8   Encyclopedia of Islam, Vol. I, 38.

CHAPTER I: THE INVISIBLE CONNECTION: THE HAMITIC MYTH

1   Quoted in, Winthrop Jordan, White Over Black
     (Chapel Hill: University of North Carolina Press,
     1968), p. 581.

2   Edith R. Sanders, "The Hamitic Hypothesis, Its
     Origin and Functions in Time Perspective,"
     Journal of African History, X (1969), 522.

3   George R. Gliddon, Ancient Egypt, Her Monuments,
     Hieroglyphics, History and Archaeology (New York:
     J. Winchester Publishers, 1844), p. 41.

4   Ibid., p. 42.

5   Sanders, op. cit., p. 527.

6   James W.C. Pennington, A Text Book of the Origin and History of the Colored People (Harford: L. Skinner, Printer, 1841), p. 5.

7   Ibid., p. 14.

8   Ibid., p. 22.

9   Rufus L. Perry, The Cushite or the Descendant of Ham (Springfield, Mass.: Wiley and Company, 1893), pp. iv-v.

CHAPTER II: AMERICAN TRAVELERS IN THE NILE VALLEY:
              IMPRESSIONS AND CONCEPTIONS

1   L.C. Wright, United States Policy Toward Egypt, 1830-1914 (New York: Exposition Press, 1969), p. 155.

2   Jasper Yeats Brinton, The American Efforts in Egypt (Alexandria: no publisher given, 1972), pp. 2-7.

3   George Bathune English (1787-1828), graduated from Harvard in 1807 and worked unsuccessfully as a minister and journalist. In 1820 he joined the U.S. Navy. Stopping in Alexandria, he resigned his commission, embraced Islam, and entered the service of Mohammed Ali Pasha. After returning from the Sudan, English joined the U.S. government as a translator in Constantinople. See Richard Hill, A Biographical Dictionary of the Sudan (London: Frank Cass and Co., Ltd., 1967), p. 120.

4   George Bathune English, A Narrative of the Expedition to Dongola and Sennar (Boston: Wells and Lilly, 1823), pp. x-xi.

5   Richard Hill, Egypt in the Sudan (London: Oxford University Press, 1966), p. 13.

6   Ibid., p. 15

7   English, op. cit., p. 47.

8   Ibid., p. 148.

9   Reverend Michael Russell, View of Ancient Egypt
     with an Outline of its Natural History (New York:
     J&J Harper, 1831), pp. 19-20.

10   The Washington Post, Sept. 30, 1979, published an
     article entitled, "Ethiopian Emergence: An Exile
     Community Stranded between Cultures," written by
     Jacqueline Trescott, a black female reporter.
     Like her 19th century white compatriots, Trescott
     was attracted to the female Ethiopian beauty.
     Says she, "The women are particularly stunning,
     the jet black hair a complementary contrast to
     small proportioned eyes, nose and lips."

11   Russell, op. cit., p. 313.

12   George Jones, Excursions to Cairo, Jerusalem,
     Damascus and Balbec (New York: Van Nostrand and
     Dwight, 1836), p. 74.

13   Ibid., p. 74.

14   Ibid., p. 75.

15   James Ewing Cooley, The American in Egypt with
     Rambles Through Arabia, Petraea and the Holy Land
     During the Years 1839 and 1840 (New York: D.
     Appleton and Company, 1842), pp. 406-7.

16   Ibid., p. 406.

17   Richard Hill, translator and editor, On the
     Frontier of Islam (London: Clarendon Press,
     Oxford, 1970), p. xxvii.

18   Cooley, op. cit., p. 414.

19   Ibid., p. 414.

20   John Lloyd Stephens, Incidents of Travel in Egypt,
     Arabia Petrea, and the Holy Land, 1st ed. (New
     York, 1838), pp. 62-3.

21   Stephen Olin, Travels in Egypt, Arabia and the
     Holy Land (reprint; New York: Arno Press, 1977),
     pp. 281-82.

22   E. Joy Morris, Notes of a Tour through Turkey,
     Greece, Egypt and Arabia Petreae (Aberdeen: George
     Clark and Son, 1847), p. 177.

23   David H. Finnie, <u>Pioneers East, The Early American Experience in the Middle East</u> (Cambridge: Harvard University Press, 1967), p. 148.

24   Bayard Taylor, <u>Journey to Central Africa</u> (New York: G.P. Putnam and Company, 1854), p. 278.

25   <u>Ibid.</u>, p. 158.

26   <u>Ibid.</u>, pp. 225-26.

27   J.V.C. Smith, <u>Pilgrimage to Egypt</u> (Boston: Gould and Lincoln, 1852), p. 318.

28   <u>Ibid.</u>, p. 318.

29   Mark Twain, <u>The Innocents Abroad</u> (special edition; New York: The Thistle Press, 1962), p. 275.

30   <u>Ibid.</u>, p. 276.

31   Alvan S. Southworth, <u>Four Thousand Miles of African Travel</u> (New York: Baker, Prait, and Company, 1875), pp. 204-05.

32   <u>Ibid.</u>, pp. 207-208.

33   <u>Ibid.</u>, pp. 209-210.

34   <u>Ibid.</u>, p. 212.

35   <u>Ibid.</u>, pp. 216-225. Most probably, Southworth brought Brilla for his pleasure, in accordance with the custom of Europeans in Khartoum at the time, and then decided to free her.

36   <u>Ibid.</u>, pp. 212-213.

37   <u>Ibid.</u>, pp. 334-335.

38   Charles Dudley Warner, <u>My Winter on the Nile</u> (Boston: Houghton, Miflin and Company, 1899), p. 254.

39   <u>Ibid.</u>, p. 255.

40   <u>Ibid.</u>, pp. 122-23.

41   Edwin De Leon, The Khedive's Egypt: The Old House of Bondage Under New Masters (London: Sampson Low, Marston, Searle and Ravington, 1877), pp. 294-95.

42   Ibid., p. 412.

43   Frederick Douglass, Life and Times of Frederick Douglass: Written by Himself (New York: Pathway Press, 1941), p. 605.

44   Ibid., p. 606.

CHAPTER III: THE MOLDING OF PUBLIC OPINION

1   Abbas, op. cit., p. 22.

2   Alan R. Booth, "The United States African Squadron, 1843-1861," in Jeffrey Butler (ed.), Boston University Papers in African History, I (Boston, 1964), p. 100.

3   "Interview with Viceroy of Egypt," New York Times, Sept. 22, 1867.

4   "Egypt, the Cotton Crop and the Slave Trade," New York Times, August 31, 1874.

5   "African Slavery," New York Times, Feb. 7, 1875.

6   "Egypt and Equatorial Africa," New York Times, Feb. 7, 1875.

7   Ibid.

8   Ibid.

9   Despatch, Elbert E. Farman United States Consul-General, Cairo, Egypt to William M. Evarts Secretary of State, Oct. 13, 1877, Diplomatic Despatches from United States Consuls in Cairo, Egypt, 1864-1906, General Records of the Department of State, Record Group 59, National Archives Microfilm Publications, T41, Roll 12. (Hereinafter National Archives Microfilm Publications will be cited as the publication and roll numbers.)

10   "The Slave Traffic in Egypt - No Sale for
        Africans and Abyssinians, But Trade in Circassians
        and Georgians Still Tolerated," New York Times,
        Nov. 11, 1877.

11   Editorial, New York Times, Dec. 24, 1877.

12   Farman was in the process of coaxing the Egyptian
        government and the Khedive to give to the city of
        New York the obelisk, "Cleopatra's Needle." Once
        the obelisk was obtained, Farman's attitude
        toward suppression of the slave trade changed
        dramatically. This point is dealt with more
        extensively in Chapter VII.

13   "Nile Valley Slave Trade," New York Times, August
        4, 1881.

14   Ibid.

15   Ibid.

16   Editorial, New York Times, Oct. 16, 1882.

17   Editorial, New York Times, Jan. 13, 1884.

18   Editorial, New York Times, Feb. 22, 1884.

19   "The Mahdi Business," New York Times, April 20,
        1884.

20   Editorial, New York Times, March 8, 1884.

21   "Gordon and Great Britain," New York Times,
        April 24, 1884.

22   "The English on the Nile," New York Times,
        Jan. 29, 1885.

23   "The War in Sudan," New York Times, Feb. 7, 1885.

24   Editorial, New York Times, Feb. 7, 1885.

25   "Irish Brigade to Aid Mahdi," New York Times,
        Mar. 2, 1885. The Irish-American groups also had
        schemes for sending money and troops to aid
        Arabi against the British in 1882, which effort
        also proved abortive. See L.C. Wright, op. cit.,
        p. 131.

26   "Anarchy in the Sudan," New York Times, July 26,
      1885.

27   "Mahdis," New York Times, July 6, 1885.

28   "England and the Soudan," New York Times, May 1,
      1884.

29   "The War in Sudan," New York Times, Feb. 7, 1885.

30   "Arab Esau and Turkish Jacob," New York Times,
      Feb. 13, 1885.

31   Editorial, New York Times, July 30, 1888.

32   Editorial, New York Times, Sept. 6, 1898.

33   "England and the Soudan, op. cit., New York Times,
      May 1, 1884.

34   "The False Prophet of the Soudan," New York Age,
      Feb. 16, 1884.

35   "African Slavery," New York Age, July 12, 1884.

36   "Slavery in Egypt," New York Age, Aug. 2, 1884.

37   "The Great War in Africa," New York Freeman,
      Feb. 7, 1885.

38   Ibid.

39   "The World in Africa," New York Freeman, Feb. 14,
      1885.

40   "Death of the Mahdi," New York Freeman, July 18,
      1885.

CHAPTER IV: MISSIONARIES AND SOLDIERS: ENVOYS OF
              MODERNIZATION

1   Andrew Watson, The American Missionary in Egypt,
      1854-1896 (2nd. ed.; Pittsburgh: United
      Presbyterian Board, 1904), p. 37.

2   Ibid., pp. 78-79.

3   L.C. Wright, op. cit., pp. 146-147.

4   Jasper Yeats Brinton, op. cit., pp. 60-61.

5   Instruction, Secretary of State William H. Seward, to United States Agent and Consul-General Charles Hale, Alexandria, Egypt, December 24, 1867, Instructions from the Department of State, Records of Foreign Service Posts of the Department of State, Record Group 84, National Archives, Washington, D.C. (Hereinafter records in the National Archives, Washington, D.C. are indicated by the symbol NA)

6   L.C. Wright, op. cit., p. 144.

7   Ibid., p. 152.

8   Andrew Watson, op. cit., pp. 51-52.

9   See Luis Awad, Tarikh al-Fikr al-Misri al-Hadith, in Arabic, (Cairo: Dar al-Hilal, 1969), pp. 118-122; and M.F. Shukry, Misr wa al-Sudan (Cairo: Dar al-Ma'rif, 1963), p. 152.

10   Watson, op. cit., p. 297.

11   Despatch, Farman to Evarts, March 29, 1877, T45, Roll 6, NA.

12   Borge Fredriksen, op. cit., p. 89.

13   "The Khalifa's Position," New York Times, June 15, 1899.

14   Ried F. Shields, Behind the Garden of Allah (Philadelphia: United Presbyterian Board of Foreign Missions, 1937), pp. 58-61.

15   Wright, op. cit., p. 73.

16   M.M. Surojoy, al-Jeish al-Misri fi al-Garn al-Tasi Ashr, in Arabic, (Cairo, 1967), p. 121.

17   Wright, op. cit., p. 74.

18   William B. Hesseltine and Hazel C. Wolf, The Blue and Grey on the Nile (Chicago: University of Chicago Press, 1961), pp. 235-36.

19   Charles Chaille-Long, <u>My Life in Four Continents</u>
      (London: Hutchinson and Company, 1912), p. 32.

20   James A. Field, <u>America and the Mediterranean
      World, 1776-1882</u> (Princeton: Princeton University
      Press, 1969), p. 394.

21   When Gordon was appointed Governor of Equatoria,
      he brought with him eight Europeans, the best
      known of whom were the American officers, Charles
      Chaille-Long and William Campbell. The crusading
      spirit of Gordon in fighting the slave trade was
      conceived from the start by Egyptian officials,
      slave traders, and Sudanese in general as a
      Christian campaign bent on destroying Islamic
      influence in Central America. Thus the two
      Americans, as well as the other American officers
      in Egypt, worked indirectly to serve the British
      embryonic emperialist designs in Central Africa.

22   William McE. Dye, <u>Moslem Egypt and Christian
      Abyssinia</u> (New York: Atkin and Prout, Printers,
      1880), p. 102.

23   <u>Ibid.</u>, p. 103.

24   <u>Ibid.</u>, p. 107.

25   Hesseltine and Wolf, <u>op. cit.</u>, p. 133.

26   <u>Ibid.</u>, p. 133.

27   Gamil Obeid, <u>al-Mudiria al-Astwaiyya</u>, in Arabic
      (Cairo, 1968), p. 394.

28   Hill, <u>A Biographical Dictionary of the Sudan</u>,
      <u>op. cit.</u>, pp. 233-34.

29   Chaille-Long, <u>op. cit.</u>, p. 67.

30   Letter, Chaille-Long to Richard Beardsley,
      Khartoum, Nov. 7, 1874, RG 59, T45, Roll 1.

31   <u>Ibid.</u>

32   Hesseltine and Wolf, <u>op. cit.</u>, pp. 70-71.

33   Brinton, <u>op. cit.</u>, p. 91.

34 Hesseltine and Wolf, op. cit., pp. 61-62.

35 William Wing Loring, A Confederate Soldier in Egypt (New York: Dodd, Mead and Company, 1884), p. 46.

36 Pierre Crabites, Americans in the Egyptian Army (London: George Rutledge and Sons, Ltd., 1938), p. 272.

37 Despatch, George Butler to Hamilton Fish, July 7, 1870, T45, Roll 6.

38 Despatch, Butler to Fish, Nov. 5, 1870, T45, Roll 6.

39 Wright, op. cit., pp. 78-79.

40 Despatch, Butler to Fish, Sept. 15, 1871, T45, Roll 6.

41 Instruction, Fish to Butler, Oct. 5, 1871, RG 84, NA.

42 Despatch, Butler to Fish, June 23, 1872, T45, Roll 6.

43 Field, op. cit., p. 386.

44 Cable, Butler to General Butler, July 13, 1872, T45, Roll 6.

45 Instruction, Fish to Butler, August 2, 1872, RG 84, NA.

CHAPTER V: THE NILE VALLEY AND THE AMERICAN CIVIL WAR

1 Despatch, Macauley to Webster, June 10, 1850, T45, Roll 2.

2 Brinton, op. cit., p. 48.

3 Despatch, Thayer to Seward, June 29, 1861, T45, Roll 3.

4 Ernest Kohlmetz, ed., The Study of American History, Vol. I (Guilford, Conn.: The Dushkin Group, Inc., 1974), p. 519.

5   Instruction, Confidential, Seward to Thayer,
     April 8, 1862, RG 84, NA.

6   Despatch, Thayer to Seward, Nov. 13, 1861, T46,
     Roll 3.

7   Fredriksen, op. cit., p. 132.

8   Instruction, Seward to Thayer, March 17, 1862,
     RG 84, NA.

9   Richard Hill, Egypt in the Sudan, 1820-1881, op.
     cit., p. 104.

10   Arnold Blumberg, "William Seward and Egyptian
     Intervention in Mexico," Smithsonian Journal of
     History (Winter, 1966-67), p. 32.

11   Despatch, Thayer to Seward, Jan. 9, 1863, T45,
     Roll 3.

12   Private letter, Thayer to Seward, Jan 12, 1863,
     T45, Roll 3.

13   Despatch, Thayer to Seward, Jan. 18, 1863, T45,
     Roll 3.

14   Despatch, Thayer to Seward, Jan. 27, 1863, T45
     Roll 3.

15   Blumberg, op. cit., pp. 32-33.

16   Despatch, Hale to Seward, August 26, 1865, T45,
     Roll 4.

17   Ibid.

18   Instruction, Seward to Hale, September 21, 1865,
     RG 84, NA.

19   Blumberg, op. cit., p. 44.

20   Despatch, Hale to Seward, Oct. 27, 1865, T45,
     Roll 4.

21   Telegram, Seward to Hale, Oct. 27, 1865, RG 84,
     NA.

22   Despatch, Hale to Seward, Nov. 13, 1865, T45,
     Roll 5.

23   Na'um Shuugair, <u>Geographyyat wa Tarikh al-Sudan</u>, in Arabic, (Beirut: Dar al-Thagafa, 1967), p. 549.

24   <u>Ibid</u>., p. 546.

25   Sherif Pasha to Hale, Nov. 16, 1865, enclosure A to despatch, Hale to Seward, Nov. 18, 1865, T45, Roll 5.

26   Instruction, Seward to Hale, Dec. 14, 1865, RG 84, NA.

27   Despatch, Hale to Seward, Jan. 17, 1866, T45, Roll 5.

28   <u>Ibid</u>.

CHAPTER VI: FROM INDIFFERENCE TO PROCRASTINATION

1   Despatch, Thayer to Seward, Jan. 27, 1863, T45, Roll 3.

2   Despatch, Thayer to Seward, March 26, 1863, T45, Roll 3.

3   Despatch, Thayer to Seward, June 4, 1863, T45, Roll 3.

4   Despatch, Thayer to Seward, June 9, 1863, T45, Roll 3.

5   Despatch, Hale to Seward, Dec. 22, 1864, T45, Roll 3.

6 · <u>Ibid</u>.

7   Despatch, Hale to Seward, June 14, 1865, T45, Roll 4.

8   Miss Finnie was the survivor of the three Dutch women whose adventurous voyages upon the White Nile in the years 1856, 1858, and 1861 had attracted the attention of geographers in all parts of the world. On the last of three voyages, Miss Finnie's mother (formerly Maid of Honor to the Queen of Holland) died, as did her aunt, a few degrees below the Equator.

9   Some European consuls-general were known to have
     enriched themselves by selling the status of
     proteges to Ottoman citizens, who were eager to
     enjoy the privileges of European powers imposed
     by the Capitulations. American consuls-general
     were not known to have sold the status of protoge,
     except for Edwin de Leon (May 24, 1853 - April
     1861), who resigned his post at the outbreak of
     the Civil War to become the Confederacy's rep-
     resentative in Europe. See M.F. Shukry, The
     Khedive Ismael and Slavery in the Sudan, 1863-
     1869 (Cairo: Libraire la Renaissance d'Egypt,
     1937).

10   Despatch, Hale to Seward, Sept. 9, 1865, T45,
     Roll 4.

11   Instructions, Seward to Hale, Oct. 31, 1865,
     RG 84, NA.

12   Despatch, A.T.A. Torbert to Hale, Havana, June 22,
     1872, T45, Roll 6.

13   Instruction, Hale to Butler, July 2, 1872, RG 84,
     NA.

14   Instruction, Hale to Butler, July 10, 1872, RG 84,
     NA.

15   Despatch, Beardsley to Hamilton Fish, Dec. 11,
     1872, T45, Roll 7.

16   Despatch, Beardsley to Fish, Dec. 12, 1872, T45,
     Roll 7.

17   Despatch, Beardsley to Fish, Dec. 15, 1872, T45,
     Roll 7.

18   Despatch, Beardsley to Fish, Jan. 3, 1873, T45,
     Roll 7.

19   Despatch, Beardsley to Fish, Feb. 24, 1873, T45,
     Roll 7.

20   Instruction, Fish to Beardsley, April 5, 1873,
     RG 84, NA.

21   Despatch, Beardsley to Fish, May 7, 1873, T45,
     Roll 7.

22   Despatch, Beardsley to Fish, May 2, 1873, T45, Roll 7.

23   Ibid.

24   Hill, A Biographical Dictionary, op. cit., pp. 305-306.

25   Instruction, Fish to Beardsley, May 31, 1873, RG 84, NA.

26   As early as 1863, the Khedive Ismail had issued orders for the protection of domestic slaves from cruelty by extending the right of maltreated slaves to be sold to another master, to that of full emancipation, giving the jurisdiction in such cases to foreign consuls. But he was forced to limit this right to cases where a full inquiry had proved maltreatment, as some consuls abused their power and manumitted as many slaves as they could. The best known example is the British Consular Agent at Mansura, who in one month in 1873 liberated 1,700 slaves.

27   Despatch, Beardsley to Fish, Sept. 16, 1873, T41, Roll 1.

28   Instruction, Fish to Beardsley, Oct. 20, 1873, RG 84, NA.

29   Despatch, Beardsley to Fish, Oct. 10, 1873, T41, Roll 1.

30   Despatch, Beardsley to Fish, Nov. 28, 1873, T41, Roll 1.

31   Despatch, Beardsley to Fish, March 7, 1874, T41, Roll 1.

32   Despatch, Beardsley to Fish, June 2, 1874, T41, Roll 1.

33   Despatch, Beardsley to Fish, Jan. 1, 1875, T41, Roll 2.

34   William McE. Dye, op. cit., p. 102.

35   Despatch, Beardsley to Fish, May 17, 1875, T41, Roll 2.

CHAPTER VII: ELBERT ELI FARMAN, AMERICAN CONSUL-
              GENERAL IN EGYPT, 1876-1881

1   Despatch, Farman to William M. Evarts, May 17,
       1876, T41, Roll 4.

2   See Elbert E. Farman, Egypt and Its Betrayal
       (New York: The Crofton Press, 1908).

3   Instruction, Evarts to Farman, March 19, 1877,
       RG 84, NA.

4   Despatch, Farman to Evarts, April 20, 1877, T41,
       Roll 4.

5   Ibid.

6   Despatch, Farman to Evarts, June 24, 1877, T41,
       Roll 4.

7   See Appendix B

8   Consolidated Treaty Series, Vol. 152, 1877-1878,
       pp. 34-39.

9   M.F. Shukry, The Khedive Ismael and Slavery in
       the Sudan, 1863-1879 (Cairo: Libraire la Renais-
       sance d'Egypt, 1937), p. 278.

10   Abbas, op. cit., pp. 95-96.

11   Despatch, Farman to Evarts, Oct. 13, 1877, T41,
       Roll 5.

12   Despatch, Farman to Evarts, June 8, 1878, T41,
       Roll 5.

13   Ibid.

14   Ibid.

15   Letter, Farman to F.W. Seward, Warsaw, New York,
       Sept. 25, 1878, T41, Roll 6.

16   Instruction, Evarts to Farman, Jan. 21, 1879,
       RG 84, NA.

17   Letter, Farman to Sherif Pasha, Cairo, April 26,
       1879, T41, Roll 6.

18   Letter, Sherif Pasha to Farman, Cairo, April 30,
      1879, T41, Roll 6.

19   Despatch, Farman to Evarts, Enclosure 4, May 1,
      1879, T41, Roll 6.

20   Despatch, Farman to Evarts, May 1, 1879, T41,
      Roll 6.

21   Letter, Farman to Seward, May 2, 1879, T41, Roll 6.

22   Despatch, Farman to Evarts, August 19, 1879, T41,
      Roll 7.

23   Instruction, Seward to Farman, August 19, 1879,
      RG 84, NA.

24   Letter, Farman to Seward, Warsaw, New York,
      Sept. 17, 1879, T41, Roll 7.

25   Despatch, Farman to Evarts, May 5, 1880, T41,
      Roll 8.

26   Despatch, Farman to Evarts, May 22, 1880, T41,
      Roll 8.

27   Despatch, Farman to Evarts, July 13, 1880, T41,
      Roll 8.

28   Ibid.

29   Ibid.

30   Despatch, Comanos to Evarts, July 23, 1880, T41,
      Roll 8.

31   Instruction, Evarts to Comanos, Oct. 7, 1880,
      RG 84, NA.

32   Despatch, Farman to James G. Blaine, May 2, 1881,
      T41, Roll 8.

33   Ibid.

34   Ibid.

35   Ibid.

36   Letter, Farman to Blaine, May 2, 1881, T41, Roll 9.

37   Ibid.

38   Abbas, op. cit., p. 121.

39   Ibid., p. 121.

40   Ibid., p. 121.

CHAPTER VIII: THE MAHDIA AND THE UNITED STATES:
                REACTIONS AND INTERPRETATIONS

1   Telegram, Pomeroy to Frederick Frelinghuysen,
    Jan. 6, 1884, T41, Roll 11.

2   Despatch, Comanos to Frelinghuysen, Jan. 8, 1884,
    T41, Roll 11.

3   Despatch, Pomeroy to Frelinghuysen, Jan. 4, 1884,
    T41, Roll 11.

4   Despatch, Pomeroy to Frelinghuysen, May 2, 1884,
    T41, Roll 11.

5   Telegram, Frelinghuysen to Pomeroy, July 17, 1884,
    RG 84, NA.

6   Despatch, Grant to Wharton, March 18, 1893, T41,
    Roll 17.

7   Fredriksen, op. cit., p. 183.

8   Despatch, Mitchell to Edwin Uhl, August 30, 1894,
    T41, Roll 20.

9   See Appendix C

10 Fredriksen, op. cit., p. 183.

11 Despatch, Long to John Hay, Jan. 20, 1899, T41,
    Roll 21.

12 Cable, Long to Hay, Sept. 4, 1898, T41, Roll 21.

13 Earl of Cromer, Modern Egypt, Vol. II (London:
    Macmillan and Company, Ltd., 1908), p. 544.

14 Despatch, Long to Hay, June 27, 1901, T41,
    Roll 22.

15 Despatch, Long to Hay, Nov. 8, 1901, T41, Roll 22.

SOURCES

Unpublished Material in the National
Archives, Washington, D.C.

United States, Department of State
Diplomatic Despatches from United States Consuls
in Alexandria, Egypt, 1835-73
General Records of the Department of State,
Record Group 59

Consular Despatch, Daniel W. Macauley United States
Consul-General, Alexandria to Daniel Webster
Secretary of State, June 10, 1850.

Consular Despatches, William S. Thayer United States
Consul-General, Alexandria to William H. Seward
Secretary of State, June 29, 1861 to June 9, 1863.

Consular Despatches, Charles Hale United States Consul-
General, Alexandria to William H. Seward Secretary
of State, August 26, 1865 to January 17, 1866.

Consular Despatches, George S. Butler United States
Consul-General, Alexandria to Hamilton Fish
Secretary of State, July 7, 1870 to June 23, 1872.

Consular Despatches, Richard Beardsley United States
Consul-General, Alexandria to Hamilton Fish
Secretary of State, December 11, 1872 to May 17,
1875.

Diplomatic Despatches from United States Consuls
in Cairo, Egypt, 1864-1906
General Records of the Department of State,
Record Group 59

Consular Despatches, Elbert E. Farman United States
Consul-General, Cairo to William M. Evarts
Secretary of State, May 17, 1876 to July 13, 1880.

Consular Despatch, H. Comanos United States Vice-Consul,
Cairo to William M. Evarts Secretary of State,
July 23, 1880.

175

Consular Despatch, Elbert E. Farman United States
    Consul-General, Cairo to James G. Blaine Secretary
    of State, May 2, 1881.

Consular Despatches, George S. Pomeroy United States
    Consul-General, Cairo to Frederick Frelinghuysen
    Secretary of State, January 6, 1884 to May 2, 1884.

Consular Despatch, H. Comanos United States Vice-Consul,
    Cairo to Frederick Frelinghuysen Secretary of
    State, January 8, 1884.

Consular Despatch, R. Grant United States Vice-Consul
    to William F. Wharton, Acting Secretary of State,
    March 18, 1891.

Consular Despatch, G. Mitchell United States Vice-
    Consul, Cairo to Edwin Uhl Secretary of State,
    August 30, 1894.

Consular Despatches, John G. Long United States Consul-
    General, Cairo to John Hay Secretary of State,
    January 20, 1899 to November 8, 1901.

United States, Department of State
Instructions from the Department of State
Records of Foreign Service Posts of the Department of
State, Record Group 84

Instructions, Secretary of State William H. Seward to
    United States Agent and Consul-General William S.
    Thayer, Alexandria, Egypt, April 8, 1862 to
    March 17, 1862.

Instructions, Secretary of State William H. Seward to
    United States Agent and Consul-General Charles
    Hale, Alexandria, Egypt, September 21, 1965 to
    December 24, 1867.

Instructions, Secretary of State Hamilton Fish to
    United States Agent and Consul-General George S.
    Butler, Alexandria, Egypt, October 5, 1871,
    August 2, 1872.

Instructions, Acting Secretary of State Charles Hale to
    United States Agent and Consul-General George S.
    Butler, Alexandria, Egypt, July 2, 1872, July 10,
    1872.

Instructions, Secretary of State Hamilton Fish to
   United States Agent and Consul-General Richard
   Beardsley, Alexandria, Egypt, April 5, 1873 to
   October 20, 1873.

Instructions, Secretary of State William M. Evarts to
   United States Agent and Consul-General Elbert E.
   Farman, Cairo, Egypt, March 19, 1877 to January 21,
   1879.

Instruction, Acting Secretary of State F.W. Seward to
   United States Agent and Consul-General Elbert E.
   Farman, Cairo, Egypt, August 19, 1879.

Instruction, Secretary of State William M. Everts to
   United States Agent and Consul-General H. Comanos,
   Cairo, Egypt, October 7, 1880.

Instruction, Secretary of State Frederick Frelinghuysen
   to United States Agent and Consul-General George P.
   Pomeroy, Cairo, Egypt, July 17, 1884.

_____ Newspapers _____

New York Age

   "The False Prophet of the Soudan," Feb. 16, 1884.
   "African Slavery," July 12, 1884.
   "Slavery in Egypt," August 2, 1884.

New York Freeman

   "The Great War in Africa," Feb. 7, 1885.
   "The World in Africa," Feb. 14, 1885.
   "Death of the Mahdi," July 18, 1885.

New York Times

   "Interview with the Viceroy of Egypt," Sept. 22,
      1867.
   "Egypt, the Cotton Crop and the Slave Trade,"
      Aug. 31, 1874.
   "African Slavery," Sept. 28, 1874.
   "Egypt and Equatorial Africa," Feb. 7, 1875.
   "The Slave Traffic in Egypt - No Sale for Africans
      and Abyssinians, But Trade in Circassians and
      Georgians Still Tolerated," Nov. 11, 1877.

"Editorial," December 24, 1877.
"Nile Valley Salve Trade," Aug. 4, 1881.
"Editorial," Oct. 16, 1884.
"Editorial," Jan. 13, 1884.
"Editorial," Feb. 33, 1884.
"Editorial," Mar. 8, 1884.
"The Mahdi Business," April 20, 1884.
"Gordon and Great Britain," April 24, 1884.
"England and the Soudan," May 1, 1884.
"The English on the Nile," Jan 29, 1885.
"The War in Soudan," Feb. 7, 1885.
"Arab Esau and Turkish Jacob," Feb. 13, 1885.
"Irish Brigade to Aid Mahdi," Mar. 2, 1885.
"Mahdis," July 6, 1885.
"Anarchy in the Soudan," July 26, 1885.
"Editorial," July 30, 1888.
"Editorial," Sept. 6, 1898.

—————————————— Books ——————————————

A. Nineteenth Century Literature:

Bacon, Lee. _Our House on the Nile_. Boston and New
    York: Houghton, Miflin and Company, 1901.
Baker, Samuel White. _The Albert N'Yanza; Great Basin
    of the Nile and Explorations of the Nile Sources_.
    Vols. I and II. 2nd ed. London: Sidgwick and
    Jackson, 1962.
Cooley, James Ewing. _The American in Egypt with Rambles
    through Petraea and the Holy Land during the Years
    1839 and 1840_. New York: D. Appleton and Company,
    1842.
De Leon, Edwin. _The Khedive's Egypt of The Old House
    of Bondage Under New Masters_. London: Sampson,
    Low, Marston, Searle and Rivington, 1877.
Douglass, Frederick. _Life and Times of Frederick
    Douglass_. reprint. New York: Pathway Press, 1841.
Dye, William McEntyre. _Moslem Egypt and Christian
    Abyssinia: or Military Service Under the Khedive,
    in His Provinces and Beyond Their Borders, As
    Experienced by the American Staff_. reprint. New
    York: Negro Universities Press, 1969.
English, George Bethune. _A Narrative of the Expedition
    to Dongola and Sennar, Under the Command of His
    Excellency Ismail Pasha, Undertaken by Order of
    His Highness Mehemmed Ali Pasha, Viceroy of Egypt_.
    1st. American ed. Boston: Wells and Lilly, 1823.

Farman, Elbert E. Egypt and its Betrayal. New York:
   The Crofton Press, 1908.
Gliddon, George R. Ancient Egypt, Her Monuments,
   Hieroglyphics, History and Archaeology. New York:
   J. Winchester Publisher, 1844.
Jones, George. Excursions to Cairo, Jerusalem, Damascus
   and Belbec. New York: Van Nostrand and Dwight,
   1836.
Legh, Thomas, Esq., M.P. Narrative of a Journey in
   Egypt. Philadelphia: M. Thomas, James Maxwell,
   Printers, 1817.
Loring, William Wing. A Confederate Soldier in Egypt.
   New York: Dodd, Mead and Company, 1884.
Morris, E. Joy. Notes of a Tour through Turkey, Greece,
   Egypt, and Arabia Petrea. Aberdeen: George Clark
   and Son, 1847.
Olin, Stephen. Travels in Egypt, Arabia and the Holy
   Land. reprint. New York: Arno Press, 1977.
Paolino, Ernest N. The Foundations of the American
   Empire: William Henry Seward and U.S. Foreign
   Policy. Cornell Univ. Press, 1973.
Pennington, James W.C. A Text Book of the Origin and
   History of the Colored People. Hartford: L.
   Skinner, Printer, 1841.
Perry, Rufus L. The Cushite or the Descendant of Ham.
   Springfield, Mass.: Wiley and Company, 1893.
Prime, William C. Boat Life in Egypt and Nubia. New
   York: Harper and Brothers, 1857.
Russell, Michael. View of Ancient Egypt with an Outline
   of its Natural History. New York: J and J Harper,
   1831.
Sawyer, George S. An Inquiry into the Origin and
   Prevalence of Slavery and the Slave Trade.
   Philadelphia: J.B. Lippincott and Company, 1858.
Schweinfurth, George. The Heart of Africa; Three Years
   Travels and Adventures in the Unexplored Region of
   Central Africa from 1868-1871. Vols. I and II.
   New York: Harper and Brothers, 1874.
Smith, J.V.C. Pilgrimage to Egypt. Boston: Gould and
   Lincoln, 1852.
Southworth, Alvan S. Four Thousand Miles of African
   Travel. New York: Baker, Prait and Company, 1875.
Stephens, John Lloyd. Incidents of Travel in Egypt,
   Arabia Petraea and the Holy Land. reprint.
   Norman: University of Oklahoma Press, 1967.
Taylor, Bayard. Journey to Central Africa. New York:
   G.P. Putnam and Company, 1854.
Twain, Mark. The Innocents Abroad. special edition.
   New York: The Thistle Press, 1962.

Warner, Charles Dudley. _My Winter on the Nile_. Boston: Houghton, Miflin and Company, 1899.

B. General History:

Ali, Abbas, Ibrahim Muhammad. _The British, the Slave Trade and Slavery in the Sudan, 1820-1881_. Khartoum, Sudan: Khartoum University Press, 1972.

Arkhurst, Frederick S., ed. _United States Policy Toward Africa_. New York: Praeger Publishers, 1975.

Booth, Alan R. "The United States African Squadron, 1843-1861," in Jeffrey Butler, ed. _Boston University Papers in African History_. New York: Praeger Publishers, 1964.

Brinton, Jasper Yeates. _The American Effort in Egypt_. Alexandria, Egypt, 1972.

Campbell, Charles S. _The Transformation of American Foreign Relations, 1865-1900_. Harper Colophon Books. New York: Harper and Row, 1976.

Chester, Edward W. _Clash of Titans; Africa and United States Foreign Policy_. Maryknoll, New York: Orbis Books, 1974.

Clendenen, Clarence; Collins, Robert; and Duignan, Peter. _Americans in Africa, 1865-1900_. Hoover Institution Studies. Stanford University: The Hoover Institution on War, Revolution, and Peace, 1966.

Collins, Robert O., ed. _Problems in African History_. Englewood Cliffs, New Jersey: Prentice-Hall, Inc., 1968.

_____. _The Southern Sudan, 1883-1898; a Struggle for Control_. New Haven: Yale University Press, 1962.

Crabites, Pierre. _Americans in the Egyptian Army_. London: George Routledge and Sons, Ltd., 1938.

_____. _Gordon: The Sudan and Slavery_. 2nd ed. New York: Negro Universities Press, 1969.

Cromer, Evelyn Baring, 1st Earl of. _Modern Egypt_. London: Macmillan and Company, 1908.

Diop, Cheikh Anta. _The African Origin of Civilization, Myth or Reality_. Mercer Cook, trans. New York: Lawrence Hill and Company, 1974.

Elkins, Stanley M. _Slavery; A Problem in American Institutional and Intellectual Life_. Chicago: The University of Chicago Press, 1968.

Field, James A., Jr. _America and the Mediterranean World, 1776-1882_. Princeton, New Jersey: Princeton University Press, 1969.

Filler, Louis. The Crusade Against Slavery, 1830-1860. New York: Harper and Brothers, 1960.

Finnie, David. Pioneers East, the Early American Experience in the Middle East. Cambridge: Harvard University Press, 1967.

Fisher, Allan G.B. and Fisher, Humphrey J. Slavery and Muslim Society in Africa. New York: Doubleday and Company, Inc., 1971.

Franklin, John Hope. From Slavery to Freedom. 4th ed. New York: Alfred A. Knopf, 1974.

Gallagher, Charles F. The United States and North Africa; Morocco, Algeria, and Tunisia. Cambridge: Harvard University Press, 1967.

Gray, Richard. A History of the Southern Sudan, 1839-1889. London: Oxford University Press, 1961.

Hesseltine, William B. and Wolf, Hazel C. The Blue and The Gray on the Nile. Chicago: University of Chicago Press, 1961.

Hill, Richard. Egypt in the Sudan, 1820-1881. London: Oxford University Press, 1959.

_____. On the Frontier of Islam. London: Clarendon Press, 1970.

Holt, P.M. A Modern History of the Sudan; from the Funj Sultanate to the Present Day. New York: Grove Press, 1961.

Irish, Marian, and Frank, Elke. United States Foreign Policy; Context, Conduct, Content. New York: Harcourt, Brace, Jovanovich, 1975.

Jordan, Winthrop D. The White Man's Burden; Historical Origins of Racism in the United States. New York: Oxford University Press, 1974.

_____. White Over Black; American Attitudes Toward the Negro, 1550-1812. Chapel Hill: University of North Carolina Press, 1968.

July, Robert W. A History of the African People. 2nd ed. New York: Charles Scribner's Sons, 1974.

Kedourie, Elie. Afghani and 'Abduh; An Essay on Religious Unbelief and Political Activism in Modern Islam. London: Frank Cass and Company, Ltd., 1966.

Kohlmetz, Ernest, ed. The Study of American History. Vols. I and II. Guilford, Conn.: The Duskin Publishing Group, Inc., 1974.

Obeid, Gamil. Al-Mudira al-Astwaiyya. Cairo, 1968.

Pratt, Julius W. A History of United States Foreign Policy. New York: Prentice-Hall, Inc., 1955.

Seligman, C.G. Races of Africa. 4th ed. Oxford Paperbacks University Series. New York: Oxford University Press, 1966.

Shields, Ried F. Behind the Garden of Allah.
    Philadelphia: United Presbyterian Board of Foreign
    Missions, 1937.
Shukry, M.F. The Khedive Ismail and Slavery in the
    Sudan, 1863-1879. Cairo: Libraire la Renaissance
    d'Egypt, 1937.
Surojy, M.M. Al-Jeish al-Misri fi al-Garn al-Tasi Ashr.
    Cairo, 1967.
Watson, Andrew. The American Missionary in Egypt, 1854-
    1896. 2nd. ed. Pittsburgh: United Presbyterian
    Board of Foreign Missions, 1904.
Wright, L.C. United States Policy Toward Egypt, 1830-
    1914. Jericho, New York: Exposition Press, 1969.

    C. References:

Bergman, Peter M. and Bergman, Mort N., ed. The
    Chronological History of the Negro in America.
    Mentor Books. New York: The New American Library,
    1969.
Encyclopedia of Islam, Vol. I, 1974.
Finley, M.I. "Slavery," International Encyclopedia of
    the Social Sciences, Vol. XIV, 1964.
Hill, Richard. A Biographical Dictionary of the Sudan.
    London: Frank Cass and Company, Ltd., 1967.
Hogg, Peter C. The African Slave Trade and its
    Suppression; A Classified Annotated Bibliography
    of Books, Pamphlets and Periodical Articles.
    London: Frank Cass and Company, Ltd., 1973.

_____ Dissertations _____

ElBashir, Ahmed E. "Confrontation Across the Sudd;
    Southern Sudan's Struggle for Freedom, 1839-1955."
    Unpublished Ph.D. dissertation, Howard University,
    Washington, D.C., 1974.

Fredriksen, Borge. "Slavery and its Abolition in
    Nineteenth Century Egypt." Unpublished Ph.D.
    dissertation, University of Bergen, Sweden, 1977.

_____ Journals _____

Blumberg, Arnold. "William Seward and Egyptian
     Intervention in Mexico." Smithsonian Journal of
     History (Winter, 1966-67), 31-48.
Brown, Leon Carl. "Color in Northern Africa."
     Daedalus (Spring, 1967), 464-82.
ElBashir, Ahmed E. "Azar Abdel Malak, the Second
     United States Consular Agent in Khartoum," in
     Arabic. Bulletin of Sudanese Studies, VI (February,
     1981), 1-30.
Farman, Elbert E. "Negotiating for the Obelisk,"
     Century, XXIV (October, 1882), 879-89.
Hales, Charles. "Consular Service and Society in
     Egypt." Atlantic Monthly, XL (1877), 280-90.
Sanders, Edith R. "The Hamitic Hypothesis; Its Origin
     and Functions in Time Perspective." Journal of
     African History, X (1969), 521-32.
Serpell, David R. "American Consular Activities in
     Egypt, 1849-63." Journal of Modern History, X
     (1938), 344-63.

_____ Treaties _____

Convention between Great Britain and Egypt for the
     Suppression of Slavery and the Slave Trade, 1895.
     Treaty Series No. 16, 1895. London: Harrison and
     Sons, 1895.

Treaties, Conventions, International Acts, Protocols
     and Agreements between the United States of
     American and other Powers, 1776-1909. Vols. I-IV.
     2nd. ed. New York: Greenwood Press, 1968.

INDEX

Abbas Pasha, 5, 62

Ahmed Chafik, 15

African Squadron, U.S.
  participation in, 46

Aggad, Mohammed Abdu Saud Bey, 8

American Council for Foreign
  Missions, 62

American missionaries
  in Egypt, 61-66, 94-95, 140
  in Sudan, 66

Anglo-Egyptian Occupation of
  Sudan - 1898, 11, 136

Arabia, 1, 5, 11, 36, 79, 125,
  126

Azar Abdel Malak, 125, 126

Baker, Sir Samuel White, 6, 8,
  40, 68, 100, 102

Baring, Sir Evelyn, 132

Beardsley, Richard, 98-109

Black Americans, 23-24, 25, 27,
  29, 46, 56-60

Black Jihadiyya, 87, 88

Butler, General Benjamin, 73, 76

Butler, George H., 73-76, 99

Cairo
  slave markets, 6, 29, 30, 31

Campbell, William P., 8

Caucasus region
  slaves imported from, 3, 137
  see also White slavery

Chahin Pasha, 74

Chaillé-Long, Charles, 8, 71-72

Circassia
  slaves imported from, 1, 30-32,
    37, 48-50, 81, 114
  see also White slavery

Cleopatra's Needle
  negotiations for, 111, 124, 130

Convention for Suppression of
  the Slave Trade between Great
    Britain and Egypt 1877; 9-10,
    48-49, 58, 114-115, 119,
    128, 145-148

Convention for Suppression of
  the Slave Trade between Great
    Britain and Egypt 1895, 11,
    136, 149-154

Cooley, James E., 31-32

Copts in Egypt, 2, 33, 34, 36,
  61, 63, 64, 65, 70, 126, 140

Cotton, 80, 81

Crabites, Pierre, 73, 168

Cuba
  alleged importation of Nile
    Valley slaves, 97-98

De Leon, Edwin, 41-42

Douglass, Frederick, 42-43

Dye, William McE., 68-70

Egypt
  American travellers, 27-43
  American officers, 66-76, 140
  American missionaries, 61-66
  Supports Union during American
    Civil War, 80-81, 93, 94
  Despatches Sudanese troops to
    Mexico, 81-90

Emin Pasha, 10

English, George Bethune, 28-29

European residents in Egypt,
  4-5, 112

Evarts, William M., 111, 117,
  124, 130

Farman, Elbert E., 48-49, 50,
  65, 111-130

Fellaheen, 1, 12, 42, 116

Finnie, Alexina, 94-95

Fish, Hamilton, 104, 105-106,
  107

French government
  solicits troops for Mexican
    campaign, 81-90

Frere, Sir Barth, 100-102

Ghazwas, 3

Gliddon, George, 22-23, 24

Gordon, Charles George
  efforts to abolish slave trade,
    8-11, 51-52, 68, 107
  evacuation of Sudan, 10, 56,
    133

Grant, James Augustus, 6

Great Britain
  efforts to abolish slave trade,
    6-11, 24, 45-46, 100, 107,
    112, 128, 134-135, 136
  Condominium Agreement and
    abolition of slavery, 11, 136

Great Britain (cont.)
  role in African Squadron and
    Mahdi Revolution, 46, 51-56,
    60, 131, 159-166
  protests despatch of Sudanese
    troops to Mexico, 86-90
Hale, Charles, 85-88, 93-98
Halim Pasha, 92, 141, 143-144
Hamitic Myth, 20-26
Islam and slavery, 1, 13-15, 51
Ismail Ayub, 9
Ismail Pasha (later Khedive)
  efforts to abolish slave trade,
    7, 8-9, 40, 41, 47, 51, 76,
    102, 108, 118-119
  expansionist policy, 40, 42,
    66-67, 68, 99, 100, 102, 104
  despatches Sudanese troops to
    Mexico, 81-90
Jews, 21, 31
Johnson, Archibald, 58
Jones, George, 30-31
Kafur, 2
Khartoum, 35, 42
Koran and slavery, 13-15
Kushites, 24, 25
Lansing, Julian, 94
Ledyard, John, 28, 34
Lincoln, Abraham, 63
Loring, William Wing, 73
Mahdi Revolution
  outbreak of, 10-11, 46, 51-52,
    131
  nature of, 131, 133-134
  slave trade during, 11
  British defeat of, 11, 164-165
  American newspaper coverage,
    51-60
  U.S. Consular despatches
    concerning, 132-134, 136-137
Manumission Bureaus in Egypt, 12,
  123, 134
Maximillian I, 81
Mexico
  Sudanese troops in, 81-90
Mohammed Abdu, 14
Mohammed Ali Pasha
  and slave trade, 3-4
  conquest of Sudan, 3-4, 28-29
  efforts to abolish slave trade,

Mohammed Ali Pasha (cont.)
  efforts to abolish slave trade,
    6, 31, 40
Morris, Edward Joy, 34
Mott, General, 74
Nile Valley
  origins of ancient civiliza-
    tions, 19-26
  American interest in, 22-26
  American travellers' percep-
    tions of, 27-43
Northern Sudan
  slavery in, 1, 1-16, 29
Nubar Pasha, 68, 90, 106, 132
Olin, Stephen, 33-34
Pennington, James C., 23-24
Perry, Rufus L., 25
Petherick, John, 6, 103
Pomeroy, George, 132, 133
Purdy Bey, E.S., 68, 74, 100,
  109
Russell, Michael (Rev.), 29-30
Said Pasha, 5, 6, 7, 62, 63, 79,
  81, 82, 90
Schweinfurth, George, 51
Seward, William, 82, 84, 85, 86,
  90
Sherif Pasha, 88, 89, 100, 118,
  120, 124, 133, 135
Shields, Ried F. (Rev.), 66
Slave revolts, 14
Slave trade Conventions
  see Convention for the
    Suppress of the Slave Trade,
    1877 and 1895
Slave trade in the Nile Valley
  nature of, 5, 151-152, 162
  efforts to abolish, 6-11, 45-
    46, 65-66, 134-135
  during Mahdist state, 11, 59,
    161
  abolition of, 9-11, 15, 136
  American accounts of, 27-43,
    46-60, 64-73
Slaves in the Nile Valley
  sources of, 1
  as soldiers, 1
  as concubines, 1, 12
  as eunuchs, 1-2, 33-34, 36
  hierarchy among, 2, 29

Slaves in the Nile Valley (cont.)
  statistics concerning, 11-12,
    38-40
  manumission of, 12, 40, 123
  American traveller's descrip-
    tions of, 27-43
  treatment of, 12, 115-116, 121-
    122, 127
Smith, Jerome, 36
Southern Sudan
  as source of slaves, 1, 3-4,
    5, 11
  opening of Sudd region, 4
Southworth, Alvan S., 38-40
Speke, John Hanning, 6
Stephens, John Lloyd, 32-33
Stone, General Charles, 67, 74-
  75
Sudan
  Anglo-Egyptian conquest, 3-4,
    11
  American travelers to, 35-43
  see also Northern Sudan;
    Southern Sudan
Sudd, 4
Taylor, Bayard, 35-36
Thayer, William, 63, 81-84, 91-
  93, 143-144
Trans-Atlantic slave trade, 1, 21
Twain, Mark, 37
United States
  American perceptions of Nile
    Valley civilization, 22-43
  slavery in, 20, 22, 36, 79
  role in African Squadron, 46
  newspaper coverage of Nile
    Valley slave trade and slavery
    46-60
  role of American missionaries,
    61-66
  American officers in Egypt, 61,
    66-76
  Civil War in, 79-80
  protests despatch of Sudanese
    troops to Mexico, 81-90
  official interest in slave
    trade convention with Egypt,
    117-120
  see also Black Americans
U.S. Consulates-General in Egypt

U.S. Consulates-General in Egypt
(cont.)
  Alexandria, 73, 74, 75, 79-109
  Cairo, 111, 130
  despatches concerning issue of
    slavery, 94-98, 98-109, 111-
    130
  despatches concerning Mahdia
    132-134, 136-137
U.S. Department of State, 74,
  75, 76, 82, 84, 87, 89, 94,
  101, 102, 103, 104, 107, 112,
  113, 117, 119, 133, 134
Warner, Charles Dudley, 41, 43
Watson, Andrew (Rev.), 64, 65
Webster-Ashburton Treaty, 46
White slavery, 1, 30-32, 37,
  48-50, 81, 114
Zubair Rahman Pasha, 9, 10,
  136